'Round the world cooking library
Italian cooking

A treasury of Italian dishes for every occasion

**Recipe contributions
by Luisa de Ruggieri,**

**Culinary editor of Italian
'Grand Hotel' magazine**

'Round the World Books Inc.•New York•Toronto

Contents

Editor	Wina Born, Dame de la Chaîne des Rôtisseurs and member of the board of the Féderation Internationale de la Presse Gastronomique
Executive editor	Ton van Es
Special consultant	Luisa de Ruggieri, culinary editor of the Italian 'Grand Hotel' magazine, author of 'La Pentola Magica' (The magic pan) and TV-cook
Food consultant, adaptation and testing of recipes	Rosemary E. McCoy, Consumer Perspective Inc., N.Y.C., N.Y. Member American Home Economics Association.
Editorial consultant	Martin Self
Photo-edition	Conny van Kasteel, Milan, Italy
Photo's pp 4 + 9	Arno Hammacher, Milan, Italy
Design and illustrations	Rosemarijn van Limburg Stirum
Created by	Meijer Pers N.V., Amsterdam the Netherlands
Typesetting by	Internationaal Zetcentrum N.V., Wormerveer, the Netherlands
Printed by	Drukkerij Meijer N.V., Wormerveer, the Netherlands
Bound by	Proost en Brandt N.V., Amsterdam, the Netherlands

Italian cuisine is among the richest and most imaginative in all of Europe. It is cooking with the same high-spirited flair for improvisation that we find in Italian music and design. An Italian kitchen is filled with flavors, colors and aromas that bring to mind the brilliant color combinations and bold design of Italian fashion. And like their fashions, Italian cooking is subtle as well as bold and varied. It was, after all, the Italians who taught the French how to cook, and a Venetian of the 16th Century who commented bitterly that 'French cooks have ruined Venetian stomachs'. The inspiration for Italian cooking begins at the màrket or behind the beaded curtain of a small cool shop in one of those narrow streets. The glowing colors and full-flavored aromas invite you to buy, and they conjure up a menu of delicacies. Silver, red, and purple-blue sea foods give off the fragrance of the deep sea, while piled up vegetables and fruit still damp from the morning dew remind you of how beautiful the land is. Herbs from warm mountain slopes mingle their scent with that of the marvelous cheeses hanging over the doors and windows of small shops. Their full-moon shapes glow in the twilight. There are bakeries full of 'pasta' in the most fantastic shapes and forms. Dark smoked hams and garlic-filled sausages fill the air with their unmistakably spicy aroma.

It is not difficult to understand how a country that has all of this to offer produces a cuisine full of fantasy and variety. The idea that Italian cooking consists exclusively of pizzas and spaghetti with tomato sauce is as strange to an Italian as chop suey and egg-rolls would be to a Chinese restaurant in Peking. When the legendary twins Romulus and Remus founded the city of Rome, Italy was a land of simple farmers who lived on bread, cheese, onions, and wine. This is still true today in the remote villages of Abruzzi and Southern Italy. But Rome grew into a rich and cosmopolitain empire that was no longer content with simple farmer's food. It imported cooks from Greece who were familiar with the refined recipes of Persia and Asia Minor. During the time of the Roman Emperors, Greek cooks were considered a status symbol. They brought the highest prices on the slave market, even higher than Greek ballad singers.

Through these cooks, Eastern refinement gradually changed and enriched the eating habits of the region. Traces of this refinement are to be found today in the full-flavored spicy sour-sweet sauces, 'agrodolce', which Italians eat with game such as rabbit, duck, and wild boar.

Early in the Middle Ages, when the Arabs ruled over Sicily, they

taught the Italian cooks the subtle art of pastry making and the technique of how to make ice cream. Ice cream manufacturing remains a specialty of the region even today. On hot days when the Sirocco wind blows off the African desert, people sometimes reduce their normally rich diet to sandwiches and lemon ice.

Arabian ships and caravans brought spices to the Mediterranean from breezy tropical islands well before the discovery of the route to the Orient. These spices were traded at the great port of Venice. Later, the first Mexican red peppers from the New World were also traded here. During the Renaissance, Italy not only led Europe in architecture, painting and music, but also in the art of cooking. At the turn of the seventeenth century, Italian cooking had evolved into more or less what it is today. Actually, it is impossible to speak of 'Italian cooking' because Italy has more than fifty million individualists who all have their own tastes and ideas about cooking, and there are few subjects to rival it in popularity—except eating. Italy has been a unified state for a little more than one hundred years and today the former independent cities, republics and principalities still conserve something of their own individuality, particularly in the

fare they serve. The diversity of foods in different areas also reflects the great variety of the Italian countryside and the wealth of things that the land produces. The cooking in Milan is quite different from that of Venice and both are markedly different from that of Umbria, Tuscany and the coast of Liguria. Rome has her own specialities, like Genoa and Naples. The odor of a kitchen in Sardinia is decidedly different from one in Sicily. And we have not even broached the subject of all the excellent Italian wines, whose makers are certainly no less individualistic than Italian cooks.

The very best place to become acquainted with Italian cooking and wines is the small 'trattoria', an informal restaurant often situated off the beaten track in the small backstreets, or in the intimate little squares of the working-class quarter, or even on the corner of a busy shopping street. The door is often nothing more than a colorful plastic curtain. There is a tile floor and wooden kitchen stools. An exuberant dark 'signora' does the cooking and the waiter knows how to combine the elegance of a ballet dancer with the courteous grace of a marquess. The clientele of these little restaurants is as varied as the food, with laborers and lawyers sitting side by side. The 'connoisseur' may even be a daily client because he knows just how good a cook the signora is.

The Italian trattoria is much more than just a commercial establishment. It is part of the way of life of a people who really appreciate their food and have come to expect the great variety of fish, fruit, vegetables, cheeses, bread and meat that comes out of the countryside. This is the same variety and quality that make a journey through Italy and through the Italian kitchens and wine cellars so rewarding and exciting. Milan, for example, is situated between the Po valley and the cool green pastures of the Alpine regions. The Milanese eat exquisite beef dishes like 'ossobucco', (beef shank served complete with bone and marrow) and rice from the humid rice fields of the Po Valley. Creamy Gorgonzola cheese and the gold-colored polenta come from this region. This is a rich and plentiful cuisine in which the butter is never spared.

From neighboring Piedmont come the subtle red wines (once very much appreciated by Julius Caesar) such as Barbera, Barolo, Nebbiolo, and the effervescent Asti Spumante, which make perfect companions for almost any dish.

It seems almost unlikely to be a coincidence that Nature always provides what is needed. If a particular region is blessed with an abundance of a certain type

FENNEL

BASIL

OREGANO

ROSEMARY

of food, there is always a suitable accompanying wine growing in the vicinity. Anyone who has seen the fish market in Venice, on an early summer morning, filled with coral-colored shrimp and deep-purple inkfish, or salt-scented 'bottarga' (caviar of red gunard) and elegant Adriatic sole, could almost anticipate that the nearby slopes of the Dolomites would grow ample quantities of twinkling fresh white wine such as the Soave and the Santa Maddelena. Venice is also a city for rice. Rice is smoked in the ink from inkfish and the result is a jetblack dish, 'riso nero' which has the odor of the deep-sea kingdom of Neptune. And to accompany the golden polenta, there is tender calf's liver which has been slowly cooked with shiny, browned onions in butter. On the other side of this boot-shaped country, there lies Genoa with the lovely Riviera coast at the top. Here people love full-flavored herbs. Genoa is famous for three piquant sauces: 'il pesto', with fresh basil, nuts and sharp sheep's cheese; 'il tocco', made from celery, onions, and mushrooms cooked in strong beef stock and white wine; and 'l'agliata', from an ancient recipe which calls for finely chopped garlic mixed with bread crumbs, olive oil, and vinegar. In every small port along the coast there is fish soup, red from tomatoes and giving off the odor of the rosemary, basil and fennel which cover the nearby mountain slopes.

High above the shining sea, on the side of the steep warm hills, lie the famous wine gardens of the 'Cinqueterre'. These vineyards are almost inaccessible, and so, in October, the grape-gatherers are brought there by boat and the full baskets of grapes are taken away with small boats. But the very fine wine that comes from these places is worth the extra effort. It is white and very dry with the hint of the bitter taste of rock fragments and the tartness of raisins. It is the perfect and delightful companion for a piquant fish soup.

Just north of the great turn of the Apennine mountains, lies the rich land of Emilia where the hogs are fattened on good corn, and where the grapevines intertwined from tree to tree resemble long ribbons of garlands. Here we find Parma, the city of the great Parmesan cheese, which is made with a bit of okra blended in. Parmesan cheese is aged for at least three years and is one of the most versatile cheeses in Italy. It is used extensively for cooking, but it has such a good taste that it is also eaten at the end of the meal to accompany that last glass of red wine. Parma can also boast a ham which is considered to be one of the best in the world. The secret of its

quality is that the hogs are fed on the same whey that is used to make Parmesan cheese, and, unlike most hams, it is hardly ever salted and is slowly dried in the fresh open air. It is eaten with a succulent, fresh melon or with cool, juicy, sweet fresh figs. Modena is also in Emilia, and a rival of Parma's skill with good pork. The specialities here are spicy sausages and exquisite stuffed 'zampone', pig's foot, whose fame has made its way all the way up to the Vatican. The story is fondly told that when pilgrims from Modena were granted an audience with Pope John XXIII His Holiness began his address to them with the words 'Ah, Modena where people eat such excellent zampone...'

The castle of Italian gastronomy is Bologna, nicknamed 'la grassa', the fat one. This is the city of goose-sausages and bologna, of green lasagna, 'lasagna verdi', and of the full-flavored red meat sauce for spaghetti 'alla Bolognese'. It is the city of an exquisite turkey dish called 'tacchino', with Parmesan cheese and ham, and mushrooms. Here Nature also furnishes an ideal wine as a companion to this cooking: Lambrusco.

It is a light effervescent red wine with a freshness that seems to have been especially designed to lighten the burden of these rich dishes.

In the Autumn, the odor of

'tartufi', white truffles, seems to float over the whole of Northern Italy. Most people would call it an unpleasant odor. But the Bolognese and the Modenese find it very pleasing, because when these raw truffles are cut over a rice or spaghetti dish and the odors mix together, there is an instant change that transforms a simple food into a noble and refined delight.

Tuscan cooking is simple. The Tuscans say that Nature is the greatest culinary artist. People here eat the best beef steak (you could say the only good beef steak) in all of Italy, 'bistecca alla fiorentina', roasted over charcoal. There is also 'pappardelle alla lepre', ribbon macaroni with a piquant rabbit sauce, and tender fragrant vegetables.

This is a region of renowned landscapes where the light is the color of glittering gold-dust and every city has served as the background for one of the paintings in the great Uffizzi Museum. But above all, Tuscany is a region of vineyards. From the tangled grapevines which wrap around the knotted elm and pear trees, comes Chianti. As long as it is young, Chianti wine has a bright red color and smells of violets. At this stage it carries the odor of the 'terracotta' earthernware vats, which themselves glow like the tiled Tuscan roofs. Chianti acquires a fiery luxuriance as it ages each year.

Umbria, the land of St. Francis of Assisi, is still a peasant land where the food is simple: in the spring, tender suckling-pig and young lamb roasted in the oven. But here there is an exquisite wine, the golden Orvieto, which can be either very dry with the taste of the volcanic ground on which it is grown, or sweet with the odor of the succulent fruit that ripens on this land in summer and autumn.

In Rome the food grows cosmopolitan again. Suckling-lamb ('abbacchio') in the springtime, and 'porchette' (suckling-pig on a spit). The Romans also eat 'saltimbocca' (literally: jump into the mouth) prepared from succulent veal with ham, and 'fritto misto', made from everything that the market could supply that day in the way of meat, fowl, and vegetables, all chopped into small pieces and fried in oil.

In the small trattoria of 'Trastevere', the picturesque old quarter across the Tiber, you can be served a marvellous mixture called 'frutti di mare', (fruit of the sea) which consists of almost everything that crawls, swims, floats, and grows in the Mediterranean Sea. All these deep-sea delicacies have a salt-sea fragrance mixed with the lightly pungent taste of white wine from Frascati.

Naples is the city of the familiar pizza, made with dark tomato sauce, and of dishes dripping with olive oil. Here there is

unrestrained fantasy in the field of pasta: maccaroncelli, fettucine, capellini, millinfanti, paternostri, cannaloni, rigatoni, perciatelli—every shape and size of strings, ribbons, little hats, sheets, pipes, bows and anything else the Neopolitans remotely fancy.

Neopolitans also eat exquisite 'frutti di mare' accompanied by the light, bitter, and somewhat volcanic tasting white wine of Ischia and the slopes of Vesuvius. One of the best known is the 'Lacrima Christi', (tears of Christ) which is named for the tears that Christ shed when he saw that the Devil would not leave even this lovely place on earth in peace.

The dark caves along the coast of Sardinia (Sardegna), shelter giant lobsters, whose color inspired the blazing red of the traditional costume of the women of Dorgolo. These woman are actually called 'arragoste', or lobsters. Sardinian shepherds, despite their rustic simplicity, are also great culinary artists: mutton which has been pressed with fragrant herbs and sprinkled with wine, is threaded onto twigs and roasted over an open fire on the ground. Roasted fowl and game which is still warm is wrapped in a sack stuffed with fragrant mountain herbs so that it can soak up their subtle tastes for a few days.

Finally, there is Sicily, the island of tuna fishers. This is where

Italy's best ice cream is made and sweet potent Marsala wine is poured over wild strawberries to create a delight, or it is mixed with beaten egg to make the lightest and most delicious dessert ever discovered: zabaglione.

We have now made our journey through Italy's kitchens, but, as many travellers have discovered, nothing is more difficult than to get an exact recipe from an Italian cook. It is no lack of good will, and certainly no shyness, but as soon as he begins to specify the ingredients he will vaguely say: 'a handful of this, a bunch of that...' But then, this is one of the secrets of the ever-present surprise in Italian cooking.

Wines

The best way to get the most pleasure out of Italian eating is to accompany your meal with a bottle or a flask of Italian wine. The Italian wines are usually not as great and refined as their French counterparts, but they provide the perfect companion for Italian food. With fish and 'antipasti' (hors d'oeuvres), serve dry white wines. These give off the aroma of herbs from warm hillside slopes and leave the same slightly sharp taste in the mouth which is typical of wines that come from old volcanic regions. With meat, serve delicious, full-bodied red wine. Italian wines taste best if they are served cool, but not icy cold.

Valle d'Aosta
Donnaz

Piemonte
Sizzano
Boca
Fara
Ghemme
Gattinara
Carema
Erbaluce di Caluso
Caluso Passito
Bubino di Cantavenna
Moscatto Naturale d'Asti
Barbera d'Asti
Barbaresco
Barbera d'Alba
Asti Spumante
Barbera del Monferrato
Brachetto d'Acqui
Nebbiolo d'Alba
Barolo

Lombardia
Valgella
Inferno
Grumello
Valtellina
Sassella
Franciacorta
Cellatica
Botticino
Riviera del Garda
Lugana
Oltrepò Pavese

Veneto
Prosecco
Breganze
Cabernet di Pramaggiore
Tocai di Lison
Recioto della Valpolicella
Valpolicella
Bardolino

Italians have been making cheese for thousands of years. The cheese that comes from the Alps is very different from that which comes from the Po valley, the Abruzzi, or from the hot South. There is creamy 'Bel Paese' and blue-striped 'Gorgonzola', sharp sheep's cheese from Rome, and, the hard, flaky 'Parmesan' cheese which is made from whey and which, when grated, is used to perk up the taste of soups, sauces, and 'pasta' dishes.

Bianco di Custoza
Recioto di Soave
Soave
Gambellara
Colli Euganei

Trentino Alto Adige
Meranese di Collina
Santa Maddalena
Terlano
Caldaro Lago di Caldaro
Teroldego Rotaliano
Trentino

Friuli Venezia Giulia
Colli Orientali del Friuli
Grave del Friuli
Collio Goriziano

Emilia-Romagna
Gutturnio dei Colli Piacentini
Lambrusco
Albana di Romagna
Sangiovese di Romagna

Tosca
Montecarlo
Rosso delle Colline Lucchesi
Chianti Montalbano
Chianti Rufina
Chianti Colli Fiorentini
Chianti Classico
Chianti Colli Senesi
Chianti Colline Pisane
Chianti Colli Aretini
Brunello di Montalcino
Bianco di Pitigliano
Elba

Umbria
Torgiano

Lazio
Orvieto

Est!Est!!Est!!!di Montefiascone
Frascati
Colli Albani
Marino
Colli Lanuvini
Velletri
Trebbiano di Aprilia
Merlot di Aprilia
Sangiovese di Aprilia
Cori

Marche
Bianchello del Metauro
Rosso Piceno
Rosso Canero
Verdicchio di Matelica
Vernaccia di Serrapetrona

Abruzzi e Molise
Montepulciano di Abruzzo

Puglia
Sansevero
Castel del Monte
Locorotondo
Martina Franca

Campania
Greco di Tufo
Taurasi
Ischia

Calabria
Ciro

Sicilia
Marsala
Etna

Sardegna
Vernaccia di Oristano

Basilicata
Aglianico del Vulture

Valla d'Aosta
Fontina

Piemonte
Gorgonzola
Grana Padano
Italico
Stracchino-Crescenza

Liguria
Fiore Sardo

Lombardia
Parmigiano Reggiano
Gorgonzola
Grana Padano
Italico
Taleggio
Mozzarella
Stracchino-Crescenza
Formaggini di Lecco

Veneto
Grana Padano
Asiago
Pressato

Friuli Venezia Giulia
Grana Padano

Emilia-Romagna
Parmigiano Reggiano
Grana Padano

Tosca
Fiore Sardo

Lazio
Pecorino Romano

Campania
Fiore Sardo

Sicilia
Ragusano
Pecorino Siciliano
Pepato

Sardegna
Pecorino Romano
Casigiolu
Fiore Sardo

Antipasti and salads

Antipasto is the Italian appetizer. Give free rein to your imagination in arranging attractive color combinations when you prepare an antipasto plate. It's fun to make up combinations which include the favorite delicacies of each individual. Usually a glass of chilled vermouth is served with the antipasto.

Antipasto

Antipasto plate

Create your own antipasto. Start with a border of lettuce leaves and sliced tomatoes. In the center arrange a variety of thinly sliced meats: prosciutto, a smoky flavored Italian ham; salami, a highly seasoned sausage; salsiccia secca, a peppery, very dry, pork sausage; capocollo, smoked pork. Garnish with quartered hard cooked eggs, anchovy fillets, radishes, green or black olives, carciofini (artichoke hearts), celery, and delicious peperoncini, a small green pepper, pickled in vinegar. Sprinkle olive oil and a little wine-vinegar over all. Pickled beets and sweet red peppers may be added for color.

Pomodori ripieni

Stuffed tomatoes

4 servings

Rice stuffing:
- 4 medium tomatoes
- $1/4$ teaspoon salt
- $1/2$ cup cooked rice
- 2 tablespoons chopped mushrooms
- 1 teaspoon capers
- 1 teaspoon parsley flakes
- $1/4$ teaspoon dried oregano
  Dash black pepper
- 1 tablespoon oil or margarine

Slice off stem ends of tomatoes; set aside. Scoop out pulp and sprinkle inside with salt; turn upside down and drain. Combine remaining ingredients; mix well. Fill tomatoes and replace tops. Brush tomatoes with oil. Place in shallow baking dish. Bake in a slow oven (325°) 15 minutes or until heated throughout. Serve hot or cold.

Tuna stuffing:
- 4 tomatoes
- $1/2$ cup tunafish, flaked
- 2–3 tablespoons mayonnaise
- 2 teaspoons lemon juice
- 1 teaspoon capers
- 1 teaspoon chopped parsley

Slice off stem ends of tomatoes; scoop out pulp; turn upside down to drain. Combine tunafish, mayonnaise, lemon juice and capers; mix well. Fill tomatoes. Garnish with mayonnaise, capers, and chopped parsley.

Scampi all'aglio

Shrimp in garlic sauce

4 servings

- 16 *large shrimp*
- $^1/_2$ *cup margarine or butter*
- $^1/_2$ *teaspoon salt*
- 3 *cloves garlic, minced*
- 2 *tablespoons chopped parsley*
- 1 *tablespoon lemon juice*
  Lemon wedges

Shell shrimp; leave on tails with their shells. Devein. Drain on paper towels. Melt margarine in large skillet over medium heat. Add salt, garlic and 1 tablespoon parsley; mix well. Sauté shrimp in single layer in margarine until shrimp turn pink. Turn shrimp. Sprinkle with lemon juice and remaining parsley. Cook 2–3 minutes longer or until shrimp are tender. Arrange shrimp on heated serving dish. Spoon drippings over shrimp. Garnish with lemon wedges.

Muscoli alla marinara

Mussels with marinara sauce

4 servings

- 24 *fresh mussels or clams*
- 1 *tablespoon oil*
- 2 *tablespoons margarine or butter*
- 1 *clove garlic, cut in half*
- $^1/_2$ *cup dry white wine*
- 2 *teaspoons chopped parsley*

Scrub mussels with brush under running water; scrape off beard, if any. Soak mussels in cold water about 2 hours to remove sand. Lift from water; wash; drain again. Pour oil in large skillet; add mussels. Place over high heat. As shells begin to open, remove mussels (leave on half shell) and keep warm. Melt margarine in small skillet. Sauté garlic just until lightly browned; remove. Add wine and parsley. Cook over high heat, stirring constantly until wine is reduced by half. Arrange mussels in wide soup dishes. Pour sauce over mussels. Garnish with lemon wedge, if desired.

Acciughe alla contadina

Anchovy salad

4 servings

- 2 *($1^3/_4$ ounce) cans anchovy fillets*
- $^1/_4$ *cup milk*
- 4 *lettuce leaves*
- 1 *small onion, cut in rings*
- 8 *stuffed olives*
- 1 *teaspoon capers*
- 4 *lemon wedges*

Soak anchovy fillets in milk about 15 minutes to remove excess salt. Rinse under running water; separate and drain on paper towel. Arrange lettuce on plates. Place anchovies, onion rings, and olives on lettuce. Sprinkle with capers. Garnish with lemon wedges.

Insalata di pollo

Chicken salad

6 servings

- 1 *cup cubed chicken*
- 2 *ounces ($^1/_3$ cup) diced Swiss cheese*
- 1 *ounce tongue or ham, cut into strips*
- 1 *cup chopped celery*
- $^1/_3$ *cup mayonnaise*
- $^1/_2$ *teaspoon salt*
- $^1/_8$ *teaspoon black pepper*
- $1^1/_2$ *teaspoons prepared mustard*
- 6 *lettuce leaves*
- 6 *slices toast*
  Pitted black olives
  Sprigs of parsley

Combine first 8 ingredients; mix lightly. Arrange lettuce leaves on toast; lightly pile salad on lettuce. Garnish with olives and parsley.

Acciughe con peperoni gialli

Anchovies with peppers

4 servings

>   2 *(1³/₄ ounce) cans anchovy
>   fillets*
> ¹/₄ *cup milk*
>   1 *green or red pepper*
>   4 *lettuce leaves*
>   2 *teaspoons capers*
>   2 *hard cooked eggs,
>   finely chopped*
>   2 *teaspoons tarragon vinegar*
> 1¹/₂ *tablespoons salad oil*
>   1 *tablespoon chopped
>   parsley*

Soak anchovy fillets in milk about 15 minutes to remove excess salt. Rinse under running water; separate and drain on paper towel. Blanch, peel and seed pepper; cut into strips. Place lettuce leaves on plates. Arrange anchovies and peppers alternately on lettuce. Sprinkle with capers; top with chopped egg. Combine vinegar and oil; sprinkle over salad. Garnish with parsley.

Sardine sott'olio alla veneta

Venetian sardines

6 servings

>   3 *(3¹/₄ ounce) cans skinned
>   and boned sardines*
>   6 *lettuce leaves*
>   1 *green pepper*
>   2 *tablespoons margarine or
>   butter*
>   1 *clove garlic, minced*
>   1 *cup (8 ounce can) tomato
>   sauce*
> ¹/₄ *teaspoon dried sage*
> ¹/₄ *teaspoon sugar
>   Dash black pepper*
>   2 *hard cooked eggs, sliced*
>   2 *teaspoons capers*

Drain sardines. Place lettuce leaves on serving dish. Arrange sardines in a radiating circular desgin on lettuce. Chill. Blanch, peel and seed pepper; cut into strips. Melt margarine in small skillet; sauté garlic. Add remaining ingredients. Cook over medium heat, stirring constantly, about 10–15 minutes. Cool. Spoon sauce over sardines. Garnish with pepper strips, egg slices and capers.

Cipolle al forno

Baked onions

6 servings

>   6 *medium onions, unpeeled*
> ³/₄ *cup salad oil*
> ¹/₄ *cup lemon juice or vinegar*
> ¹/₂ *teaspoon dry mustard*
> ¹/₄ *teaspoon salt*
> ¹/₈ *teaspoon black pepper*
>   1 *green pepper*

Slice off tops and bottoms of onions; place onions in shallow baking pan. Bake in a moderate oven (350°) about 25 minutes. Cool slightly. Remove skins. Combine remaining ingredients; blend well. Pour over onions. Chill. Blanch, peel and seed pepper. Cut into strips. Garnish onions with pepper strips before serving.

Cipolle farcite con purea di tonno

Tuna-stuffed onions

6 servings

>   1 *cup dry white wine or water*
>   1 *cup vinegar*
>   1 *clove garlic, minced*
>   1 *teaspoon salad oil*
>   1 *bay leaf*
> ¹/₄ *teaspoon dried thyme*
>   6 *medium onions, peeled*
>   1 *cup (7 ounce can) tunafish*
> ¹/₃ *cup chopped green olives*
>   1 *tablespoon chopped parsley*

Combine wine, vinegar, garlic, oil, bay leaf and thyme in saucepan. Add onions. Bring to a boil; simmer about 20 minutes or until onions are tender. Cool. Remove onions. Chill. Cook liquid mixture over high heat until mixture is reduced by half. Strain and cool. Mix together tunafish and olives. Carefully remove centers from onions. Fill onions with tuna mixture. Spoon sauce over onions. Garnish with parsley.

Prosciutto con melone

Prosciutto with melon

Cut 1 honeydew or cantelope in half; remove seeds and peel. Cut into individual portions. Serve with rolls of paper-thin prosciutto (about ¹/₄ pound for 1 melon). To keep ham fresh and moist, cover tightly with plastic wrap until ready to serve. Serve with freshly ground pepper or pass the pepper mill at table. Westphalian or Virginia ham may be substituted for prosciutto.

Cavolfiore all'aceto

Cauliflower in vinegar

6 servings
1 medium cauliflower
1 cup vinegar
1 cup water
1 clove garlic, cut in half
2 teaspoons dried basil
3 tablespoons salad oil
1 tablespoon lime or lemon juice
1 teaspoon parsley flakes
1 teaspoon chopped chives
¹/₄ teaspoon salt
Dash black pepper

Wash and trim cauliflower; break into flowerets. Cook covered in a small amount of boiling, salted water 10–15 minutes; drain. Combine vinegar, water, garlic and basil; bring to a boil. Pour over cauliflower. Cover and chill. Just before serving drain cauliflower, Combine remaining ingredients and pour over cauliflower.

Prosciutto con fichi

Prosciutto with figs

Arrange paper-thin slices of prosciutto on serving dish. Serve with well chilled, fresh, ripe figs (or substitute chilled, drained canned figs). To keep ham fresh and moist, cover tightly with plastic wrap until ready to serve. Westphalian or Virginia ham may be substituted for prosciutto.

Insalata al tonno

Tunafish salad

4 servings
1 tablespoon salad oil
1 teaspoon vinegar
1 teaspoon chopped parsley
¹/₄ teaspoon salt
Dash black pepper
1 large potato, cooked and diced
12 lettuce leaves
2 tomatoes, sliced
2 hard cooked eggs, sliced
1 (7 ounce) can tunafish
8 rolled anchovies
8 green or black olives

Combine oil, vinegar, parsley, salt and pepper; pour over potatoes; toss lightly. Arrange lettuce leaves in individual salad bowls. Place tomato slices on lettuce, then potatoes, and then egg slices; top with tunafish. Garnish with anchovies and black olives.

Peperoni dolci all'olio e prezzemolo

Sweet peppers with oil and parsley

4 servings

 4 red or green peppers
 3 tablespoons salad oil
 3 tablespoons chopped parsley
 1 tablespoon lemon juice
 1 clove garlic, minced
 $1/4$ teaspoon salt
 4 lettuce leaves, optional
   Dash black pepper
   Capers

Blanch, peel and seed peppers; cut into strips. Combine oil, parsley, lemon juice, garlic, and salt. Arrange lettuce leaves on individual plates. Place pepper strips on lettuce. Pour oil mixture over peppers. Garnish with capers.

Pomodori all'italiana

Italian tomato salad

6 servings

18 *small plum tomatoes or*
6 *medium tomatoes*
3 *tablespoons salad oil*
1 *tablespoon vinegar*
$^1/_2$ *teaspoon salt*
$^1/_2$ *teaspoon dried basil*
Freshly ground black pepper
1 *tablespoon finely chopped parsley*

Cut plum tomatoes in half or slice larger tomatoes. Mix remaining ingredients; blend well. Pour over tomatoes. Chill about 1 hour.

Mozzarella in carrozza

Mozzarella cheese sandwich

4 servings

8 *slices white bread*
$^1/_2$ *pound mozzarella cheese, sliced*
$^1/_4$ *teaspoon salt*
Dash black pepper
2 *eggs, slightly beaten*
$^1/_2$ *cup milk*
4 *tablespoons margarine or butter*

Trim crusts from bread. Place sliced cheese on 4 slices bread. Sprinkle with salt and pepper; top with remaining bread. Mix egg and milk. Dip sandwiches into egg mixture. Melt 2 tablespoons margarine in skillet over medium heat. Sauté sandwiches in margarine until golden brown on both sides, adding more margarine when necessary. Serve hot.

Insalata mista di verdura

Tossed vegetable salad

6 servings

$^1/_2$ *medium head lettuce*
$^1/_2$ *medium head romaine*
2 *scallions, chopped*
1 *stalk celery, chopped*
$^1/_2$ *cup sliced fresh mushrooms*
6 *radishes, thinly sliced*
$^1/_2$ *cup pitted, ripe olives, sliced*
6 *tablespoons salad oil*
2 *tablespoons wine vinegar*
$^1/_4$ *teaspoon garlic salt*
$^1/_4$ *teaspoon salt*
$^1/_4$ *teaspoon dry mustard*
Dash black pepper

Tear greens into bite-size pieces. Combine greens, scallions, celery, mushrooms, radishes and olives in large salad bowl. Combine remaining ingredients; blend well. Pour over greens; toss lightly until greens are well coated. Serve immediately.

Insalata di spinaci

Spinach salad

6 servings

1 *pound fresh spinach*
$^1/_2$ *teaspoon salt*
1 *clove garlic, minced*
6 *tablespoons salad oil*
2 *tablespoons wine vinegar*
Dash black pepper
2 *scallions, chopped*
2 *hard cooked eggs, cut in wedges*
1 *tomato, cut in wedges*

Wash and trim spinach; drain well; tear into bite-size pieces. Sprinkle salt into bottom of salad bowl; mash garlic into salt until well blended. Add the vinegar, oil and black pepper. Mix well. Add spinach and toss lightly. Garnish with eggs and tomato.

Antipasti literally means: before the meal. It is the Italian equivalent of appetizers. The Italians talent for improvisation and their colorful imagination is most vividly seen in their preparation of the antipasti. When you order this course in one of the large luxurious restaurants of Rome, Florence, Bologna, or Milan, the waiter arrives at your table pushing a three-story cart filled with large and small dishes containing every possible type of fish, both shell and scale. There are sausages, many kinds of ham, vegetables, salads, miniature pizzas, and golden brown fritters with the most surprising contents. Then, with plate and fork in hand, the competent waiter begins to dish out all that fills your heart's desire. You will want to taste nearly everything! Each appetizer looks more delicious and more interesting and exciting than the one before. It takes real will power to limit yourself to a reasonable serving and to think of the rest of the meal that is still to come. Antipasti contain everything, and all possible ingredients can be used in their preparation. Italians probably acquired their almost uncontrolled imagination and sense of endless variety in making antipasti from the Arabians, who ruled over Sicily and a great part of southern Italy in the Middle Ages. All those small spicy delicacies remind one of the 'meze' which come from the countries of the Middle East. There are, on the whole, three large categories of Italian appetizers: fish, meat, and vegetables. Fish appetizers can either be prepared from fresh fish or from one of the many canned fish products such as anchovies in olive oil, tuna in olive oil, squid in piquant sauce, mussels in sauce, or sardines in oil. However, the spicy taste and the vivid colors of the sauces must not cover up the delicate and sweet flavor nor the lovely red color of the shell fishes such as crab, shrimps, or prawns. Meat appetizers often consist of raw, spicy, smoked ham. Sometimes it is combined with fresh sweet melon, or with juicy ripe figs. A filling, spicy garlic sausage, or cooked calf's tongue and pork fillet can be exquisite. Vegetable appetizers are made out of all that the season can offer fresh or whatever can be taken from the pots and jars containing asparagus, cauliflower, artichoke hearts, mushrooms, bell peppers, beans, fennel, green peas, and almost everything else that has been marinated in olive oil, wine-vinegar, or lemon juice. Olives, both green and black, must not be absent from the assortment; and neither must hard-boiled eggs, radishes, capers, and pickles.

All these different delicacies are prepared and served on individual dishes, but all arranged side by side on a large tray. They are eaten with bread and a good measure of one of the dry, cool, straw-yellow Italian wines which both quenches thirst and whets the appetite.

Spiedini

Skewer delight

6 servings

- 2 *chicken breasts*
- 4 *hot Italian sausages*
- 6 *chicken livers*
- 6 *slices bacon, cut in half*
- 18 *large mushroom caps*
- 4 *tablespoons melted margarine or butter*
   Dash paprika

Cut chicken breasts into 6 pieces each; sausages into 3 pieces; chicken livers in half. Wrap bacon around chicken livers; secure with toothpick. Thread meats and mushrooms on small skewers. Brush mushrooms and chicken well with melted margarine. Sprinkle chicken with paprika. Broil, 3″ from heat turning once, until done about 5 minutes each side. To serve as main course double recipe.

Soups

In Italy, the noon-time meal begins with antipasto, but the evening meal begins with soup. The soup is made of a full-bodied chicken or meat broth, carefully skimmed of the fat; a handful of fresh vegetables adds flavor and texture. A generous amount of grated Parmesan cheese is sprinkled on at the table and sometimes, as in the 'zuppa pavese', a poached egg floats on top. A favorite soup is the 'pasta in brodo'. This is made by cooking any of the many thin spaghetti or noodle pastas in clear broth. Thick soups such as minestrone contain not only cooked pasta but also a variety of vegetables and meats. The typical taste of the Italian minestrone is obtained by first frying the vegetables in bacon fat and then cooking them in broth. Grated cheese is sprinkled on generously, and it isn't too much to say that a good minestrone is a meal in itself. In Tuscany a few drops light-green olive oil from the Tuscan hillside round out the flavor. In Genoa no soup is complete without basil and garlic. In Rome, Pecorino cheese is used to sprinkle over the soup, rather than Parmesan. Pecorino is a sharp sheep's cheese from the Albanese hills. Mint is often used as a garnish. Oregano is a favorite herb in Naples.

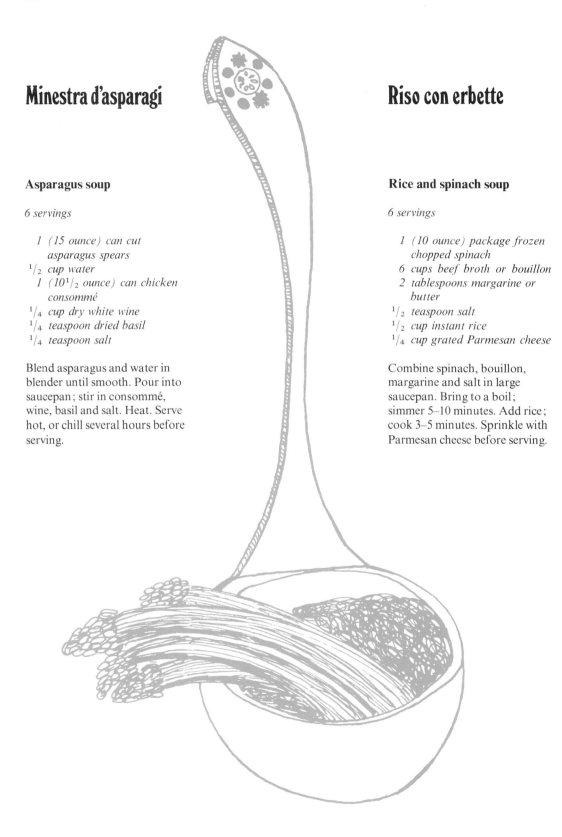

Minestra d'asparagi

Asparagus soup

6 servings

- 1 (15 ounce) can cut asparagus spears
- $^1/_2$ cup water
- 1 (10$^1/_2$ ounce) can chicken consommé
- $^1/_4$ cup dry white wine
- $^1/_4$ teaspoon dried basil
- $^1/_4$ teaspoon salt

Blend asparagus and water in blender until smooth. Pour into saucepan; stir in consommé, wine, basil and salt. Heat. Serve hot, or chill several hours before serving.

Riso con erbette

Rice and spinach soup

6 servings

- 1 (10 ounce) package frozen chopped spinach
- 6 cups beef broth or bouillon
- 2 tablespoons margarine or butter
- $^1/_2$ teaspoon salt
- $^1/_2$ cup instant rice
- $^1/_4$ cup grated Parmesan cheese

Combine spinach, bouillon, margarine and salt in large saucepan. Bring to a boil; simmer 5–10 minutes. Add rice; cook 3–5 minutes. Sprinkle with Parmesan cheese before serving.

Minestra di carciofi

Artichoke soup

6 servings

- 3 tablespoons margarine or butter
- 1 small onion, chopped
- 1 (10 ounce) package frozen artichoke hearts
- 4 cups water
- 1 thin strip lemon peel
- 4 chicken bouillon cubes
- $^1/_2$ cup instant rice
- 1 egg, slightly beaten
- $^1/_4$ cup grated Parmesan cheese

Melt margarine in large saucepan. Sauté onion and artichoke in margarine until onion is transparent. Stir in water, lemon peel and bouillon cubes. Cook over medium heat, stirring occasionally, about 10–15 minutes. Remove lemon peel. Add rice; cook 3–5 minutes. Slowly stir a small amount of hot mixture into beaten egg; return to hot mixture; blend well. Sprinkle with Parmesan cheese before serving.

Minestra con broccoli

Broccoli soup

6 servings

- 3 tablespoons margarine or butter
- 1 clove garlic, cut in half
- 2 (10 ounce) packages frozen chopped broccoli
- 6 cups hot water
- 4 chicken bouillon cubes
- 1 tablespoon tomato paste
- $^1/_2$ teaspoon salt
  Dash black pepper
  Croutons

Melt margarine in large saucepan over medium heat. Brown garlic in margarine; remove. Add broccoli; cook just until heated. Add water, bouillon cubes, tomato paste, salt and pepper. Cook 5–10 minutes. Force through fine sieve or blend smooth in blender. Cook over medium heat, stirring occasionally until heated, about 10–15 minutes. Serve with croutons.

Minestrone freddo

Cold minestrone

8 servings

- 2 tablespoons olive oil
- 1 medium onion, chopped
- 3 stalks celery, chopped
- $^1/_2$ teaspoon dried basil
- 3 potatoes, cubed
- 4 cups hot water
- 4 beef bouillon cubes
- 1 medium zucchini, chopped
- 2 (10 ounce) packages frozen mixed vegetables

Heat oil in large saucepot. Sauté onions, celery and basil until onion is transparent. Add potatoes, water, and bouillon cubes. Simmer, covered, 30 minutes. Add zucchini and mixed vegetables. Cook until heated throughout, about 15–20 minutes. Chill. Serve chilled with hot garlic bread.

Minestra di pasta e ceci

Chick pea soup

6 servings

- 2 tablespoons margarine or butter
- 2 scallions, chopped
- 1 tablespoon parsley flakes
- $^1/_2$ teaspoon oregano
- 1 (1 pound) can tomatoes
- 1 (16 ounce) can chick peas
- 2 cups water
- 1 beef bouillon cube

Melt margarine in large saucepan. Sauté scallions, parsley and oregano in margarine over medium heat, 2–3 minutes. Add remaining ingredients. Cook over medium heat, 5–10 minutes, or until heated throughout.

Minestra d'orzo

Barley soup

6 servings

- $^1/_4$ pound bacon, diced
- 1 small leek, chopped
- 2 stalks celery, chopped
- 2 carrots, sliced
- 3 medium potatoes, cubed
- $^1/_2$ cup barley
- 1 tablespoon chopped parsley
- $^1/_2$ teaspoon salt
  Dash black pepper
- 2 quarts beef bouillon

Cook bacon until crisp in large heavy saucepot. Remove bacon; pour off drippings, returning 3 tablespoons to pot. Add vegetables; cook just until celery softens slightly. Add remaining ingredients and bacon. Cook over medium heat, stirring occasionally, until barley is tender, about 1 hour.

Brodo con tortellini alla bolognese

Bouillon with tortellini Bolognese style

8–10 servings

4 cups sifted flour
6 eggs, slightly beaten
1 tablespoon salad oil
1 teaspoon salt
$^3/_4$ pound ground pork
$^1/_4$ pound ground beef
$^1/_4$ pound ground ham
1 egg yolk
$^1/_4$ cup grated Parmesan cheese
$^1/_4$ teaspoon nutmeg
12 cups beef bouillon
1 tablespoon tomato paste

Place flour in large bowl; add eggs, oil, and salt. Mix until dough can be gathered into a ball. Place dough on lightly floured board; knead until firm but elastic and smooth. Place dough in slightly dampened cloth; let stand $^1/_2$ hour. Brown meat in large skillet; stir in ham. Remove from heat; blend in egg yolk, cheese and nutmeg. Form into 1″ balls. Roll out on lightly floured board, to $^1/_8$″ thickness. Cut into 2″ circles; place one meatball in center of each circle. Fold dough over; forming a crescent. Moisten edges; seal with fork. Cover. Let stand 24 hours in a cool place. Just before serving bring bouillon to a boil; stir in tomato paste. Drop tortellini into bouillon; cook 15 minutes or until done. Serve with additional Parmesan cheese.

Zuppa pavese

Pavia soup

4 servings

2 (10$^1/_2$ ounce) cans chicken consommé
1 soup can water
$^1/_4$ cup margarine or butter
$^1/_4$ cup grated Parmesan cheese
4 slices toast, crusts removed
4 poached eggs

Combine consommé and water; bring just to a boil. Reduce heat; simmer. Mix together margarine and cheese; blend well. Spread cheese mixture on toast. Place 1 slice toast in each soup bowl; top with egg. Ladle hot consommé into bowls. Serve immediately

Zuppa di lenticchie

Lentil soup

6 servings

1 pound lentils
2 quarts water
$^1/_4$ pound bacon, finely diced
1 medium onion, finely chopped
1 clove garlic, minced
1$^1/_2$ teaspoons salt
$^1/_2$ teaspoon dried oregano

Rinse lentils. Combine lentils and water in large saucepot. Bring to a boil; simmer about 1$^1/_2$ hours or until lentils are soft. Cook bacon until crisp in skillet. Remove bacon; pour off drippings, returning 3 tablespoons to skillet. Add remaining ingredients and bacon. Cook over medium heat, stirring constantly until onion is transparent. Press lentils through a fine sieve or blend smooth in blender. Add bacon mixture; stir well.

Stracciatella

Stracciatella

4 servings

4 cups chicken bouillon
2 eggs, slightly beaten
2 tablespoons flour
$^1/_4$ cup grated Swiss cheese
2 tablespoons grated Parmesan cheese
$^1/_4$ teaspoon salt
Dash nutmeg
4 slices bread, toasted
Chopped parsley

Bring 3 cups bouillon to a boil; reduce heat; simmer. Combine eggs and flour; stir in cheeses, nutmeg, and salt. Gradually stir in remaining bouillon. Stir a small amount of hot mixture into egg mixture. Slowly stir into hot bouillon. Reduce heat. Continue to cook, stirring constantly, until mixture thickens, about 3–4 minutes. Remove crusts from toast; cut into quarters; float on soup. Garnish with chopped parsley.

This very characteristic soup comes from Genoa. It is prepared with another Genoese speciality, 'pesto' (which literally means pounded or crushed), a mixture of aromatic ingredients, green in color, because of the spinach and basil used in its preparation.

Minestrone alla genovese

Genoese minestrone

8 servings

$1/4$ cup olive oil
1 clove garlic, minced
1 onion, finely chopped
1 leek, washed and diced
1 tablespoon parsley
$1/2$ teaspoon dried thyme
1 tablespoon tomato paste
3 medium tomatoes, peeled, seeded, and chopped
2 stalks celery, chopped
2 carrots, diced
2 potatoes, diced
1 (10 ounce) package frozen string beans
6 cups water
6 beef bouillon cubes
1 cup elbow macaroni or ditali
$1^1/2$ cups drained, cooked, kidney beans
Pesto, optional
Grated Parmesan cheese

Heat olive oil in large saucepot. Add garlic, onion, leek, parsley and thyme; cook until onion is transparent. Add tomato paste, tomatoes, celery, carrots, potatoes, string beans, water and bouillon cubes. Simmer covered, about 1 hour. Bring to a boil; add macaroni; cook until tender, about 8–10 minutes. Add beans; heat. Serve with pesto and Parmesan cheese.

For the pesto:

1 (10 ounce) package frozen chopped spinach well drained
1 teaspoon dried basil
3 cloves garlic, minced
1 tablespoon parsley flakes
4 tablespoons salad oil
2 tablespoons margarine or butter
$1/4$ cup grated Parmesan cheese

Combine all ingredients in top of blender; blend smooth. Or combine all ingredients in sauce pan; bring to a boil; press through fine sieve. Stir 1 or 2 tablespoons pesto into each bowl of minestrone.

Minestra alla romana

Roman soup

6 servings

1 tablespoon margarine or butter
1 medium onion, chopped
1 clove garlic, minced
2 quarts beef bouillon
1 tablespoon tomato paste
$1/2$ teaspoon salt
Dash black pepper
$1/4$ teaspoon dried basil
$1/4$ pound fine noodles, broken into 2" pieces

Melt margarine in large heavy saucepot; sauté onion and garlic in melted margarine until onion is transparent. Add bouillon, tomato paste, salt, pepper and basil; stir well. Bring to a boil; then simmer 10 minutes. Add noodles. Continue to cook, over medium heat, until noodles are done, about 5–6 minutes.

Minestrone all'italiana

Minestrone

12 servings

6 slices bacon, finely diced
1 large onion, chopped
2 carrots, diced
$1/2$ pound ($1^1/2$ cups) string beans, cut up
1 small head cauliflower, separated
$1/4$ pound ham, cut into strips
1 (10 ounce) package frozen lima beans
2 quarts beef bouillon
2 medium zucchini, chopped
1 pound spinach, finely chopped
$1/4$ pound spaghetti, broken into 2" pieces
2 tablespoons chopped parsley
1 teaspoon salt
Dash black pepper
Grated Parmesan cheese

Cook bacon until crisp in large heavy saucepot. Remove bacon; pour off drippings, returning 3 tablespoons to saucepot. Sauté onion until slightly transparent. Add carrots, string beans, cauliflower, ham, lima beans and bouillon. Cook over medium heat until vegetables are tender, about 30 minutes. Add remaining ingredients and cook until spaghetti is done, about 8–10 minutes. Serve with grated Parmesan cheese.

Risi e bisi is a specialty of Veneto, the northeastern part of Italy. Veneto lies to the north-west of Venice. The success of this soup depends on the quality of the peas. The fresher and the more tender they are, the better.

Brodo con gnocchetti malfatti

Broth with dumplings

8 servings

1 recipe green dumplings page 42 or
1 recipe spinach and Ricotta dumplings page 42
8 cups chicken or beef bouillon
1 tablespoon tomato paste
Grated Parmesan cheese

Prepare dumplings according to recipe directions. Bring bouillon to a boil; stir in tomato paste. Drop dumplings into broth; cook until dumplings come to the surface, about 8–10 minutes. Serve immediately with grated Parmesan cheese.

Brodo con tagliarini

Bouillon with tagliarini

8 servings

4 (10$^1/_2$ ounce) cans beef or chicken consommé
2 soup cans water
1 tablespoon tomato paste
$^1/_2$ cup finely chopped mushrooms
8 ounces (4 cups) tagliarini or fettucini noodles

Combine consommé and water; bring to a boil. Stir in tomato paste and mushrooms. Add noodles; cook until noodles are tender, about 10 minutes.

Minestra di 'risi e bisi'

Rice and pea soup

4 servings

2 (10$^1/_2$ ounce) cans chicken consommé
1 soup can water
6 ounces ham, cut in strips
2 teaspoons onion flakes
1 (10 ounce) package frozen peas or
2 cups fresh peas

Combine soup, water, ham, and onion in saucepan; bring to a boil. Reduce heat; add peas. Cook about 7–10 minutes or until peas are tender.

Minestra di 'risi e luganese' alla veneta

Rice soup Venetian style

6 servings

2 (10$^1/_2$ ounce) cans tomato rice soup
2 soup cans water
2 cups peas
$^1/_4$ cup chopped celery
1 teaspoon parsley flakes
4 strips bacon, cooked and crumbled

Combine soup, water, peas, celery and parsley in saucepan; stir well. Heat; stir now and then. Garnish with crumbled bacon.

Pasta

'Pasta' identifies the multitude of products made from semolina or flour and water and then dried in various shapes and forms, each one of which has its own, mostly very descriptive name. Each region of Italy has its special shape, the variations limited only by the imagination. Italian grocery stores carry all types of dried pasta, the pasta secca. It's a tempting adventure to make your own pasta fresca, the fresh or homemade pasta. However, if you prefer, ready-made pasta (available at all supermarkets) may be substituted. Pasta is a regular part of the Italian menu. It is usually served as a first course. At lucheon a modest dish of pasta serves as the main course, followed by cheese and fruit. Each recipe given in this book calls for a particular pasta. It is the one suited for the recipe. However, a similar pasta may be substituted. Remember though, to substitute only pasta of like size. The following guide has been prepared for your convenience.

acimi di pepe: 'peppercorns' tiny pieces of round or square pasta; used in soups.

agnolotti: round *ravioli*, filled with meat.

anelli and **anellini:** 'rings' and 'little rings' (for soups).
cannelloni: flat squares of pasta rolled around a stuffing.
cappelletti: 'little hats', flat or round squares with filling.

cavatelli: a short curled noodle, formed like a shell.
conchiglie: shaped like sea shells. Sometimes called *maruzze, maruzelle* or *conchigliette.*

ditali: 'thimbles'; macaroni cut in short lengths, about $1/4$ inch in diameter and $1/2$ inch long.
ditalini: same shape as ditali but cut in $1/4$ inch lengths. Used in soups.
farfalle, farfallette or **farfalloni:** 'butterflies'. Small and large ribbon bows.

fettuccine, fettuccelle: 'ribbons'. About $1/4$ inch wide. Easy to make as a fresh pasta.

fusilli: a spiral, curly spaghetti, twisted like a corkscrew.

lasagne: a very wide flat pasta used most often in baked dishes. Also sold with one or two sides rippled.

maccheroni (or macaroni): hollow or pierced pasta products. There are more than 20 sizes of hollow pastas. Most often used is *mezzani*, a smooth, curved tubular pasta about 1 inch long and $1/4$ inch in diameter. Other sizes are *bucatini, mezzanelli, ziti, zetoni, cannelle,* and *tufoli.*

mafalde: long twisted ribbon noodles.
ravioli: pasta squares, stuffed with eggs, vegetables or cheese. Other sizes are called *anolini, anolotti* or *raviolini* (small ravioli).

rigatoni: large, ribbed, tubular pasta cut into 3 inch lengths.

spaghetti: pasta dried in long, thin, round strands, as distinguished from the *macaronis* (round but hollow) and noodles like *lasange* (flat). Listed as *spaghetti's* are *capellini, fedelini, vermicelli, spaghettini,* and *spaghettoni.*

tagliatelle: narrow egg noodles, not different from the fettucine. The tagliatelle is $3/4$ inch wide in the home-made version. The 4 names in this family ranging from $3/4$ inch to $1/8$ inch are *tagliatelle, tagliolette, tagliolini* and *tagliarini.*

tortellini: 'small twists', to be stuffed.

vermicelli: Very thin *spaghetti.* Vermicelli is sold not only in straight rods, but also sometimes 15 or 20 strands are twisted to form a bow knot.

Pasta all'uovo

Pasta dough made with eggs

2 pounds pasta

    4 *cups sifted flour*
    6 *eggs*
    5 *teaspoons salad oil*
$1^1/_2$ *teaspoons salt*

Place flour in large bowl; add
eggs, oil, and salt. Mix until
dough can be gathered into a
ball. Place dough on lightly
floured board; knead until firm
but elastic and smooth. Place
dough in slightly dampened
cloth; let stand $^1/_2$ hour. Divide
dough into quarters; roll out
dough on lightly floured board
to $^1/_8''$ thickness. Fold dough
over into a long roll; cut dough
into desired size.
Fettucini: cut rolled dough into
        $^1/_4''$ strips
Tagliatelle: cut rolled dough
        into $^3/_8''$ strips
Tagliarini: cut rolled dough
        into $^1/_8''$ strips
Lasagne: cut dough into strips
        2″ wide and 8″ long
Manicotti: cut dough into
        $4 \times 4^1/_2''$ squares
Cover cut dough; let dry 1 hour
before cooking. To cook pasta
bring 6–8 quarts water to a rapid
boil. Add 2 tablespoons salt and
1 teaspoon salad oil Add pasta
a few pieces at a time. As soon
as pasta rises to the surface test
for doneness. Pasta should still
be firm ('al dente' or some
resistance to the bite). Drain.

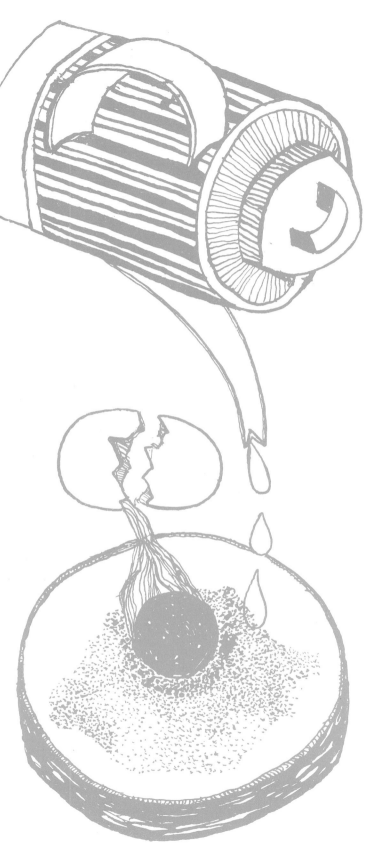

Cappelletti

Little hats in tomato sauce

6 servings

    1 *recipe pasta all'uova*
      page 29
$1^1/_2$ *cups ground cooked*
      chicken
    1 *cup Ricotta cheese*
    2 *eggs*
$^1/_4$ *cup bread crumbs*
    1 *tablespoon chopped chives*
    1 *teaspoon salt*
$^1/_2$ *teaspoon dried basil*
    2 *cups tomato sauce*
      page 43 or
    1 *(16 ounce) jar spaghetti*
      sauce with mushrooms

Prepare dough according to
directions on page 29. Roll
dough out into 2 sheets $^1/_8''$
thick. Cover. Combine chicken,
cheese, eggs, bread crumbs,
chives, salt and basil; mix well.
Place a teaspoonful of filling at
$1^1/_2''$ intervals on one sheet of
dough. Cover with second sheet.
Cut out squares or circles with
knife or cookie cutter. Moisten
edges; seal with fork. Shape so
that dough resembles a hat.
Cook in rapidly boiling salted
water, about 10 minutes or until
tender. Drain well. Serve with
hot sauce.

Ravioli

Manicotti

Ravioli

6 servings

3$^1/_2$ cups sifted flour
$^1/_4$ teaspoon salt
  3 eggs, slightly beaten
  2 tablespoons soft margarine
    or butter
$^1/_2$ cup lukewarm water
  1 cup cooked ground
    chicken
  1 cup well drained
    spinach
  2 eggs, slightly beaten
$^1/_2$ cup bread crumbs
$^1/_4$ cup grated Parmesan
    cheese
  2 teaspoons parsley flakes
  1 clove garlic, minced
$^1/_2$ teaspoon salt
$^1/_4$ teaspoon black pepper
  2 cups tomato sauce
    page 43 or
  1 (16 ounce) jar meatless
    spaghetti sauce

Place flour and salt in large bowl; add 3 eggs, margarine and water. Mix until dough can be gathered into a ball. Place dough on lightly floured board; knead until firm but still smooth and elastic. Cover; let stand 15 minutes. Meanwhile, combine chicken, spinach, 2 eggs, bread crumbs, cheese, parsley, garlic, salt and pepper; mix well. Divide dough in half; roll each half out to $^1/_8$″ thickness. Place a teaspoonful of filling at 1$^1/_2$″ intervals on one sheet of dough. Cover with second sheet. Cut apart into squares or rounds

with a knife or cookie cutter. Moisten edges; seal edges with a fork. Allow to dry 1 hour. Cook in batches in 6 quarts boiling salted water, about 5–10 minutes or until done; drain. Serve with hot sauce.

Macaroni muffs

4 servings

  1 pound manicotti tubes or
 22 (4″) squares home-made
    pasta all'uova page 29
  2 cups Ricotta cheese
  2 eggs, slightly beaten
$^1/_4$ pound ham, ground
$^1/_2$ cup grated Parmesan
    cheese
  1 tablespoon chopped chives
  2 teaspoons parsley flakes
  1 teaspoon salt
$^1/_4$ teaspoon black pepper
  2 cups tomato sauce
    page 43 or
  1 (16 ounce) jar marinara
    sauce

Cook manicotti tubes according to package directions, or cook squares of home-made pasta in 6 quarts boiling salted water, about 4 minutes. Remove with slotted spoon; drain well on cheesecloth. Combine Ricotta cheese, eggs, ham, Parmesan cheese, chives, parsley, salt and pepper. Mix well. Fill manicotti tubes with filling, or spread filling on cooked dry pasta squares; roll up tightly. Moisten edges and seal tightly. Spoon small amount of sauce on bottom of buttered 13$^1/_2$″ × 8$^3/_4$″ × 2″ baking pan. Place manicotti in baking pan. Pour remaining sauce over manicotti. Bake in a moderate oven (375°) about 20–25 minutes or until hot and bubbly.

Lasagne alla cacciatora

Lasagne hunters' style

8–10 servings

     4 *tablespoons margarine or
        butter*
     4 *tablespoons olive oil*
     1 *large onion, chopped*
     2 *cloves garlic, minced*
 $1/_4$ *pound mushrooms, chopped*
     1 *(2$^1/_2$–3 pound) chicken,
        cooked, boned and cubed*
 $1/_4$ *pound chicken livers,
        chopped*
 $1/_4$ *pound ham, diced*
     1 *teaspoon salt*
 $1/_4$ *teaspoon black pepper*
 $1/_2$ *cup red wine*
     3 *cups tomato puree*
     1 *teaspoon dried basil*
 $1/_2$ *teaspoon dried rosemary*
     1 *teaspoon parsley flakes*
    10 *ounces lasagne noodles*
 $1/_2$ *cup grated Parmesan
        cheese*

Melt margarine in large skillet
over medium heat; add oil.
Sauté onion, garlic and
mushrooms in hot oil mixture
until onion is transparent. Add
chicken, chicken livers and ham.
Cook about 2–3 minutes.
Sprinkle with salt and pepper;
add wine. Continue to cook
until wine is reduced by half.
Skim off excess fat. Add tomato
puree and herbs; cook 25–30
minutes. Cook lasagne
according to recipe or package
directions; drain well. Butter a
$13^1/_2'' \times 8^3/_4'' \times 2''$ baking dish.
Arrange alternate layers of
noodles and meat mixture,
ending with meat mixture.
Sprinkle with Parmesan cheese.
Bake in a moderate oven (350°)
about 25–30 minutes or until
heated throughout.

Lasagne alla Paola

Lasagne Paula's style

8–10 servings

     1 *pound sweet Italian sausage*
     1 *pound ground beef*
     1 *clove garlic, minced*
     1 *tablespoon dried basil*
     1 *teaspoon salt*
     1 *(1 pound) can tomatoes*
     2 *(6 ounce) cans tomato
        paste*
 $1/_2$ *cup dry red wine*
    10 *ounces lasagne noodles*
     2 *eggs*
     3 *cups Ricotta or cottage
        cheese*
 $1/_2$ *cup grated Parmesan
        cheese*
     2 *tablespoons parsley flakes*
     1 *teaspoon salt*
 $1/_8$ *teaspoon black pepper*
     1 *pound mozzarella cheese,
        thinly sliced*

Brown meat in heavy skillet;
spoon of excess fat. Add garlic,
basil, 1 teaspoon salt, tomatoes,
tomato paste and wine. Simmer,
uncovered, about 30 minutes,
stirring frequently. Cook
lasagne according to package
directions; drain. Beat eggs; add
Ricotta, Parmesan cheese,
parsley, salt and pepper. Blend
well. Layer half the lasagne in
a buttered $13^1/_2'' \times 8^3/_4'' \times 2''$
baking dish; spread with half
the Ricotta mixture. Add half
the mozzarella cheese; then half
the meat sauce. Repeat. Bake in
a moderate oven (375°) 30
minutes or until bubbly.

Lasagne al forno

Baked lasagne

8–10 servings

   3 *tablespoons margarine or
      butter*
   2 *(4 ounce) cans sliced
      mushrooms*
$^1/_4$ *pound ham, cut in strips*
   1 *tablespoon parsley flakes*
   3 *cups Bolognese sauce
      page 43 or*
   3 *(8 ounce) cans beef gravy
      or Bolognese sauce*
$^1/_2$ *cup heavy cream or
      evaporated milk*
  10 *ounces lasagne noodles*
$1^1/_2$ *cups grated Parmesan
      cheese*

Melt margarine in large skillet;
sauté mushrooms, ham and
parsley flakes. Add Bolognese
sauce. Simmer uncovered, 15–20
minutes. Cook lasagne
according to package directions;
drain. Layer half the lasagne
noodles in a buttered
$13^1/_2'' \times 8^3/_4'' \times 2''$ baking dish.
Stir cream into sauce; spread
half the sauce over the noodles;
sprinkle with half the grated
cheese. Repeat. Bake in a
moderate oven (375°) about 30
minutes or until bubbly.

Lasagne con le vongole rosse

Lasagne with red clam sauce

8–10 servings

$^1/_4$ *cup margarine or
      butter*
   2 *cloves garlic, minced*
   3 *(8 ounce) cans minced
      clams, drained*
   1 *(29 ounce) can tomatoes,
      drained*
   2 *eggs, slightly beaten*
   2 *cups Ricotta cheese*
$^1/_2$ *cup grated Parmesan
      cheese*
   2 *tablespoons parsley flakes*
   1 *teaspoon salt*
$^1/_2$ *teaspoon black pepper*
   1 *pound mozzarella
      cheese, sliced*
  10 *ounces lasagne noodles*

Melt margarine in skillet; sauté
garlic and clams until garlic is
lightly browned. Stir in
tomatoes. Cook over medium
heat, stirring occasionally,
about 15–20 minutes. Combine
eggs, Ricotta, Parmesan cheese,
parsley, salt and pepper; blend
well. Layer half the lasagne
noodles in a buttered
$13^1/_2'' \times 8^3/_4'' \times 2''$ baking dish;
spread with half the clam
mixture; top with half the
mozzarella cheese. Repeat. Bake
in a hot oven (375°) about 30
minutes or until hot and bubbly.

Spaghetti con prosciutto e uova

Spaghetti with ham and eggs

4 servings

   1 *pound spaghetti*
   4 *tablespoons margarine or
      butter*
$^1/_2$ *pound ham, diced*
   2 *eggs, slightly beaten*
   2 *tablespoons cream,
      optional*
   2 *tablespoons chopped
      chives*
$^1/_2$ *teaspoon salt*
$^1/_8$ *teaspoon black pepper*
$^1/_2$ *cup grated Parmesan
      cheese*

Cook spaghetti according to
package directions. Melt
margarine in skillet; sauté ham
until lightly browned. Drain
spaghetti well; return to pot.
Immediately add ham, eggs,
cream, chives, salt and pepper;
toss lightly. (Heat from the
spaghetti cooks eggs). Add
Parmesan cheese; toss lightly.

Spaghetti con acciughe

Spaghetti with anchovies

4 servings

   1 *pound spaghetti*
$^1/_2$ *cup margarine or
      butter*
$^1/_4$ *cup olive oil*
   2 *cloves garlic, minced*
   2 *($1^3/_4$ ounce) cans
      anchovies with oil*
$^1/_2$ *cup chopped black olives*
   1 *teaspoon capers*
$^1/_4$ *teaspoon dried oregano*
$^1/_4$ *teaspoon dried mint
      Grated Parmesan cheese*

Cook spaghetti according to
package directions. Melt
margarine in saucepan; add oil;
heat. Add garlic, anchovies,
olives, capers, oregano and
mint. Cook 2–3 minutes, stirring
frequently, to break up
anchovies. Drain spaghetti.
Pour sauce over spaghetti; toss
lightly. Serve immediately with
grated Parmesan cheese.

Spaghetti con salsa di pollo

Spaghetti with chicken sauce

4 servings

  6 tablespoons margarine or
     butter
  1 medium onion, chopped
  1 small green pepper,
     chopped
$^1/_4$ pound mushrooms, sliced
  2 pimentos, diced
  1 ($10^1/_2$ ounce) can cream
     of chicken soup
  1 cup milk
  2 tablespoons sherry wine,
     optional
$^1/_2$ teaspoon salt
     Dash nutmeg
  2 cups cooked chicken, cubed
$^1/_4$ cup bread crumbs
  1 pound spaghetti

Melt 4 tablespoons margarine in
heavy saucepot. Sauté onion,
pepper and mushrooms in
margarine until onion is
transparent. Stir in pimento,
soup, milk, sherry, salt and
nutmeg; blend well. Add
chicken; simmer 5–10 minutes.
Melt remaining margarine in
small skillet; add bread crumbs;
stir gently. Cook spaghetti
according to package directions;
drain well. Pour sauce over
spaghetti; top with bread
crumbs.

Spaghetti all'aglio

Spaghetti with garlic sauce

4 servings

  1 pound spaghetti
$^1/_2$ cup margarine or
     butter
$^1/_2$ cup olive oil
  4 cloves garlic, minced
$^1/_4$ cup finely chopped parsley
$^1/_2$ teaspoon dried basil
$^1/_2$ teaspoon dried oregano
$^1/_2$ teaspoon salt
     Dash black pepper
     Grated Parmesan cheese

Cook spaghetti according to
package directions. Melt
margarine in heavy saucepot;
add oil; heat. Sauté garlic until
lightly browned. Stir in parsley,
basil, oregano, salt and pepper.
Drain spaghetti well; return to
pot. Add sauce; toss lightly.
Serve with grated Parmesan
cheese.

Spaghetti alla napoletana

Spaghetti Neapolitan style

4 servings

  6 slices bacon, diced
  1 medium onion, chopped
  1 pound ground beef
  1 (1 pound) can tomatoes
  1 (8 ounce) can tomato sauce
  1 tablespoon tomato paste
  1 teaspoon sugar
$^1/_2$ teaspoon dried basil
$^1/_2$ teaspoon dried oregano
  1 pound spaghetti

Fry out bacon in heavy
saucepot. Sauté onion in bacon
fat until transparent. Drain off
excess fat. Brown meat. Add
tomatoes, tomato sauce, tomato
paste, sugar, basil and oregano;
stir well. Simmer 15–20 minutes.
Cook spaghetti according to
package directions; drain well.
Serve sauce over spaghetti.

Spaghetti marinara

Spaghetti with marinara sauce

4 servings

  4 tablespoons olive oil
  2 onions, chopped
  2 cloves garlic, minced
  2 anchovy fillets
  1 (29 ounce) can tomatoes
$^1/_2$ cup dry white wine
$^1/_2$ teaspoon salt
$^1/_4$ teaspoon dried oregano
$^1/_4$ teaspoon sugar
  1 pound spaghetti
     Grated Parmesan cheese

Heat oil in heavy saucepot;
sauté onions and garlic in oil
until onions are transparent.
Add anchovies; stir to break up
anchovies. Add tomatoes, wine,
salt, oregano and sugar. Simmer
25–30 minutes. Meanwhile,
cook spaghetti according to
package directions; drain well.
Pour sauce over spaghetti;
sprinkle with grated Parmesan
cheese.

Spaghetti con le vongole

Spaghetti with white clam sauce

4 servings

$1/2$ cup margarine or
    butter
$1/4$ cup salad oil
  3 cloves garlic, minced
  2 (8 ounce) cans minced
    clams, drained
$1/4$ cup finely chopped parsley
$1/4$ teaspoon dried basil
$1/4$ teaspoon dried oregano
$1/4$ teaspoon salt
    Dash black pepper
  1 pound spaghetti
    Grated Parmesan cheese

Melt margarine in saucepot;
add oil; heat. Sauté garlic and
clams in hot oil mixture over
medium heat, 2–3 minutes. Stir
in parsley, basil, oregano, salt
and pepper. Simmer 5–10
minutes. Cook spaghetti
according to package directions;
drain well. Return to pot; add
sauce; toss lightly. Serve with
grated Parmesan cheese.

Spaghetti al tonno

Spaghetti with tuna sauce

4 servings

  3 tablespoons margarine or
    butter
  1 medium onion, chopped
  1 clove garlic, minced
$1/4$ pound mushrooms
    sliced
  2 anchovy fillets, optional
  2 (7 ounce) cans tunafish
  2 (8 ounce) cans tomato
    sauce
$1/4$ cup sliced green
    olives
  1 pound spaghetti

Melt margarine in heavy
saucepot. Sauté onion, garlic
and mushrooms until onion is
transparent. Add anchovies and
tunafish; stir in tomato sauce.
Simmer 15–20 minutes. Cook
spaghetti according to package
directions; drain well. Pour
sauce over spaghetti. Garnish
with olive slices.

Tagliarini con fegatini

Noodles and chicken livers

4 servings

$1/2$ cup margarine or
    butter
  1 medium onion, chopped
$1/2$ pound mushrooms,
    sliced
$1/4$ cup flour
$1/2$ teaspoon salt
$1/8$ teaspoon black pepper
  1 pound chicken livers
$1/2$ cup Marsala wine
$1/4$ cup water
  1 pound tagliarini or
    medium noodles

Melt margarine in large skillet;
sauté onion and mushrooms in
margarine until onion is
transparent. Combine flour, salt
and pepper. Cut chicken livers
in half; dredge with flour. Add
chicken livers and all the flour
mixture to skillet. Cook until
chicken livers are lightly
browned. Stir in wine and water.
Cook over low heat, stirring
occasionally, until chicken livers
are cooked, 5–10 minutes. Cook
noodles according to package
directions; drain well. Serve
chicken livers over noodles.

Tagliatelle ai funghi

Tagliatelle and mushrooms

4 servings

  1 pound tagliatelli or
    fettucini noodles
$1/2$ cup margarine or
    butter
$1/4$ cup salad oil
  1 pound mushrooms, sliced
  2 teaspoons parsley flakes
  1 teaspoon salt
$1/4$ teaspoon black pepper
    Grated Parmesan cheese

Cook noodles according to
package directions. Melt
margarine in heavy saucepot;
add oil; heat. Sauté mushrooms
in hot oil mixture; stir in
parsley, salt and pepper. Drain
noodles well; return to pot. Add
mushroom sauce; toss lightly.
Serve with grated Parmesan
cheese.

Fettucine con salsa di prezzemolo

Fettucini with parsley sauce

4 servings

    1 pound fettucini or
      thin noodles
$^1/_2$ *pound unsalted*
      margarine or butter
$^1/_2$ *cup heavy cream*
$^1/_2$ *cup chopped parsley*
    1 teaspoon dried basil
$^1/_2$ *teaspoon salt*
    Dash black pepper
    2 cups grated
      Parmesan cheese

Cook noodles according to package directions. Slice half the margarine into warm bowl or chafing dish; add cream, parsley, basil, salt and pepper. Drain noodles quickly; pour into bowl. Slice in remaining margarine. Toss gently, turning noodles, over and over, until noodles are well coated. Add cheese; toss lightly until cheese coats noodles. Serve immediately.

Fusilli con fegatini

Fusilli with chicken livers

4 servings

    4 tablespoons margarine or
      butter
    1 medium onion, chopped
$^1/_4$ *pound mushrooms,*
      sliced
    1 pound chicken livers
    2 tablespoons flour
$^1/_2$ *cup dry red wine*
    2 cups Bolognese sauce
      page 43 or
    2 (8 ounce) cans beef gravy or
      Bolognese sauce
$^1/_2$ *teaspoon salt*
$^1/_4$ *teaspoon black pepper*
    1 pound fusilli or
      spaghetti

Melt margarine in heavy saucepot; sauté onion and mushrooms until onion is transparent. Cut chicken livers in half; dredge with flour. Add chicken livers and all the flour to saucepot; cook until chicken livers are lightly browned. Stir in red wine; cook, stirring constantly, until wine is reduced by half. Stir in Bolognese sauce, salt and pepper. Simmer 15–20 minutes. Cook fusilli according to package directions; drain well. Serve chicken livers over hot fusilli.

Farfalle al tonno

Farfalle and tunafish

6 servings

    2 ($10^1/_2$ ounce) cans
      mushroom soup
    1 soup can milk
    1 (4 ounce) can sliced
      mushrooms
    1 tablespoon chopped chives
    2 teaspoons onion flakes
$^1/_2$ *cup sliced green olives*
    8 ounces American cheese,
      shredded
    2 (7 ounce) cans tunafish,
      drained
    1 large tomato, sliced
    12 ounces farfalle (or bows)
      cooked and drained

Combine soup, milk, mushrooms, onion flakes, and chives; mix well. Stir in olives, cheese and tunafish. Layer half the farfalle in buttered $2^1/_2$ quart casserole; then a layer of half the tuna mixture. Repeat. Arrange sliced tomatoes on top. Bake in a moderate oven (350°) about 25–30 minutes.

Mostaccioli con carciofi

Mostaccioli with artichoke hearts and Ricotta cheese

6 servings

    1 pound mostaccioli or
      elbow macaroni
    3 tablespoons margarine or
      butter
    3 tablespoons salad oil
    1 small onion, sliced
    3 frozen or canned
      artichoke hearts
    1 cup dry white wine
$^1/_4$ *teaspoon black pepper*
    1 cup Ricotta or
      cottage cheese
$^1/_2$ *cup milk*
    2 egg yolks
$^1/_4$ *cup grated Parmesan*
      cheese
    1 teaspoon salt
$^1/_4$ *cup finely chopped*
      parsley

Cook macaroni according to package directions. Melt margarine in large skillet over medium heat; add oil. Sauté onion until transparent. Quarter artichoke hearts; add to saucepan. Stir in wine and pepper. Cook over medium heat until wine is reduced by half. Meanwhile, combine Ricotta cheese, milk, egg yolks, Parmesan cheese and salt; beat until well blended. Drain macaroni well; place in warmed serving dish. Add cheese mixture and artichoke mixture, toss lightly until well mixed. Garnish with finely chopped parsley.

Ziti alla carbonara

Anolini

Tortelli di ricotta

Sformato di maruzzelle

Ziti alla carbonara

4 servings

- $^1/_2$ *pound bacon, diced*
- *1 onion, chopped*
- $^1/_2$ *cup dry white wine*
- *1 pound ziti*
- *3 eggs, slightly beaten*
- $^1/_4$ *cup grated Parmesan cheese*
- $^1/_2$ *teaspoon salt*
  Dash black pepper

Cook bacon until crisp in heavy saucepot. Remove bacon; drain off drippings, returning 2 tablespoons to pot. Sauté onion in drippings until just transparent; add wine; cook until wine is reduced by half. Cook ziti according to package directions; drain well; return to pot. Add bacon, onion mixture, eggs, Parmesan cheese, salt and pepper. Toss lightly, until ziti is well coated. Serve immediately.

Anolini

6 servings

- *1 recipe Pasta all'uova page 29*
- $^1/_2$ *pound Italian sweet sausage*
- *1 pound ground beef*
- *1 medium onion, chopped*
- *2 carrots, grated*
- *1 stalk celery, finely chopped*
- *1 cup bread crumbs*
- *3 eggs, slightly beaten*
- *1 teaspoon salt*
- $^1/_4$ *teaspoon nutmeg*
- $^1/_4$ *teaspoon black pepper*
- *8 cups beef bouillon or water*
  Grated Parmesan cheese

Prepare dough according to direction on page 29. Roll dough out into 2 sheets $^1/_8''$ thick. Break up sausage. Brown sausage and meat in large skillet. Add onion, carrot and celery; cook until onion is transparent. Drain off excess fat. Remove from heat; stir in bread crumbs, eggs, salt, nutmeg and pepper; mix well. Place a teaspoonful of filling at $^1/_2''$ interval on one sheet of dough. Cover with second sheet. Cut out squares or circles with a knife or cookie cutter. Moisten edges; seal with fork. Cover; let stand 1 hour. Bring bouillon to a boil; add anolini; cook about 10 minutes or until tender. Serve in small amount of bouillon, topped with grated cheese.

Tortelli with Ricotta filling

4 servings

- *1 recipe pasta all'uova page 29*
- *1 (10 ounce) package frozen chopped spinach*
- $1^1/_2$ *cups Ricotta cheese*
- *3 eggs*
- *3 tablespoons grated Parmesan cheese*
- $^1/_2$ *teaspoon salt*
- $^1/_4$ *teaspoon nutmeg*
- $^1/_8$ *teaspoon black pepper*
- $^1/_2$ *cup margarine or butter*
- $^1/_4$ *cup grated Parmesan cheese*
- $^1/_4$ *teaspoon dried sage*

Prepare dough according to directions on page 29. Roll dough out into 2 sheets $^1/_8''$ thick. Cover. Cook spinach; drain well. Combine spinach, Ricotta cheese, eggs, Parmesan cheese, salt, pepper and nutmeg; mix well. Place a teaspoonful of filling at $1^1/_2''$ intervals on one sheet of dough. Cover with second sheet. Cut out squares or circles with a knife or cookie cutter. Moisten edges; seal with fork. Cover; let stand 20 minutes. Cook in rapidly boiling salted water for 10 minutes or until tender. Drain well. Melt margarine; stir in remaining Parmesan cheese and sage. Pour margarine mixture over tortelli before serving.

Maruzelle mold

4 servings

- $^1/_2$ *pound maruzzelle (shell) macaroni*
- *4 tablespoons margarine or butter*
- *4 tablespoons grated Parmesan cheese*
- *2 eggs, slightly beaten*
- $^1/_2$ *pound ground beef*
- *1 (4 ounce) can sliced mushrooms*
- *4 chicken livers*
- *2 tablespoons flour*
- $^1/_2$ *cup dry red wine or bouillon*
- *1 (8 ounce) can tomato sauce*
- $^1/_2$ *teaspoon salt*
  Dash black pepper
- *1 (10 ounce) package frozen peas, cooked*

Cook macaroni according to package directions; drain. Add margarine, cheese, and eggs; toss lightly to blend. Spoon mixture into well buttered $1^1/_2$ quart ring mold. Set mold in pan of hot water. Bake in a moderate oven (375°) 20 minutes. Brown meat in large skillet; add mushrooms; cook 2–3 minutes. Cut chicken livers in half; dredge with flour. Add chicken livers to skillet; cook until browned. Add wine; cook until mixture begins to thicken. Stir in tomato sauce, salt and pepper. Simmer 15–20 minutes. Unmold macaroni mold; fill center with meat mixture. Place peas around bottom of mold.

Risotto milanese

Rice Milanese

6 servings

- 6 *tablespoons margarine or butter*
- 1 *medium onion, finely chopped*
- 2 *cups raw rice*
- $^1/_4$ *pound ground beef*
- $^1/_2$ *cup dry white wine*
- 6–7 *cups hot beef bouillon*
- $^1/_8$ *teaspoon saffron, optional*
- $^1/_4$ *cup grated Parmesan cheese*

Melt 2 tablespoons margarine in heavy saucepot. Sauté onion in margarine until just transparent. Add rice; cook 1–2 minutes, stirring constantly, or until rice grains become slightly opaque and glisten slightly. Add meat. Cook, stirring constantly, until lightly browned. Add wine; bring to a boil; cook until wine is reduced by half. Add 2 cups bouillon. Cook until almost all liquid is absorbed. Stir in 2 more cups bouillon; cook, stirring occasionally until all liquid is absorbed. Stir saffron into 2 cups bouillon; let steep several minutes; pour over rice. Cook until liquid is completely absorbed. If rice is not tender, add remaining bouillon, $^1/_2$ cup at a time. Continue to cook and stir until rice is soft. Stir in remaining margarine and cheese. Serve immediately.

Risotto genovese

Genoese Rice

6 servings

- $^1/_2$ *pound ground pork*
- 1 *medium onion, chopped*
- 1 *clove garlic, minced*
- $^1/_2$ *cup dry white wine*
- 2 *cups raw rice*
- $^1/_2$ *teaspoon dried thyme*
- $^1/_2$ *teaspoon dried mint*
- $^1/_2$ *cup brown sauce (page 43) or*
- $^1/_2$ *cup beef gravy*
- 6 *cups water*
- 6 *beef bouillon cubes*
- 6 *artichoke hearts, quartered*
- 4 *tablespoons margarine or butter*
- $^1/_4$ *cup grated Parmesan cheese*

Brown meat in large heavy saucepot. Sauté onion and garlic in margarine until onion is transparent. Add wine; cook until wine is reduced by half. Add rice, thyme, mint, brown sauce, water and bouillon cubes; stir until cubes are dissolved. Cook, covered, over medium heat until liquid is absorbed and rice is tender, about 20 minutes. Stir now and then. If rice is not tender, add a little water; cook until rice is soft. Stir in margarine and butter.

Risotto con legumi

Risotto with vegetables

6 servings

- 2 *cups raw rice*
- 1 *(10 ounce) package frozen mixed vegetables*
- 2 *tomatoes, peeled, seeded and chopped*
- 1 *medium onion, chopped*
- $^1/_2$ *teaspoon salt*
- $^1/_8$ *teaspoon black pepper*
- $^1/_4$ *cup margarine or butter*
- 4 *beef bouillon cubes*
- 1 *quart hot water*
- *Grated Parmesan cheese*

Place rice, vegetables, tomatoes, onion, salt and pepper in $2^1/_2$ quart casserole; mix well. Place pats of margarine on rice mixture. Dissolve bouillon cubes in hot water; stir into rice mixture. Cover. Bake in a moderate oven (375°) about 30 minutes. Remove cover; stir; bake another 30 minutes. Sprinkle with grated Parmesan cheese; bake 5–10 minutes longer or until cheese is golden brown.

Risotto con fegetini

Risotto with chicken livers

6 servings

4 tablespoons margarine or
  butter
$^1/_2$ pound chicken livers
1 small onion, chopped
$^1/_2$ cup finely chopped
  mushrooms
1 tablespoon parsley flakes
1 cup raw rice
$2^1/_2$ cups hot water
2 chicken bouillon cubes
$^1/_2$ teaspoon salt
  Grated Parmesan cheese

Melt margarine in heavy
saucepot. Brown chicken livers
in margarine; remove; chop.
Sauté onion, mushrooms, and
parsley in margarine until onion
is transparent. Add rice; cook,
stirring constantly, about 2
minutes. Add water and
bouillon cubes; stir until cubes
are dissolved and well blended.
Cover. Cook over low heat until
liquid is absorbed and rice is
tender, about 20 minutes; stir
now and then. If rice is not
tender, add a little water; cook
until rice is soft. Stir in chicken
livers. Serve immediately with
grated Parmesan cheese.

Risotto verde

Green risotto

6 servings

1 (10 ounce) package frozen
  chopped spinach
2 tablespoons margarine
1 medium onion, chopped
1 clove garlic, minced
2 cups raw rice
4 cups hot water
4 chicken bouillon cubes
$^1/_2$ teaspoon salt
  Grated Parmesan cheese

Drain spinach well. Combine
spinach, margarine, onion and
garlic in heavy saucepan. Bring
to a boil; cook, stirring
constantly, about 5 minutes.
Press through fine sieve or blend
smooth in blender; return to
pan. Add rice, water, bouillon
cubes and salt; stir until cubes
are dissolved. Cover. Cook over
low heat until liquid is absorbed
and rice is tender, about 20
minutes. Stir now and then. If
rice is not tender, add a little
water; cook until rice is soft.
Serve immediately with grated
Parmesan cheese.

Risotto al limone

Lemon rice

6 servings

4 tablespoons margarine or
  butter
1 cup raw rice
$2^1/_2$ cups hot water
1 chicken bouillon cube
2 strips lemon peel $^1/_2$" wide
$^1/_2$ teaspoon salt
2 eggs, slightly beaten
$^1/_2$ cup grated Parmesan cheese

Melt margarine in heavy
saucepan. Add rice; cook 1–2
minutes, stirring constantly until
rice grains become opaque and
glisten slightly. Add water,
bouillon cube, lemon peel and
salt; stir until cube is dissolved.
Cover. Cook over low heat
about 10 minutes. Remove
lemon peel; stir; continue to
cook until liquid is absorbed
and rice is tender, about 20
minutes. If rice is not tender,
add a little water; cook until rice
is soft. Combine eggs and grated
cheese; stir into rice. Cook over
low heat 2–3 minutes.

Ziti alla carbonara

Sformato di tortelli

Polenta

Polenta

8 servings

$1^1/_2$ cups cornmeal
3 cups water
1 teaspoon salt

Combine cornmeal and 2 cups water in heavy saucepan; mix well. Stir in remaining water and salt. Bring to a boil, stirring constantly. Be sure cornmeal does not lump. Continue to cook, stirring constantly, until mixture is so thick, spoon will stand up, unsupported, in the middle of the pan. Pour into a buttered $1^1/_2$ quart bowl or mold. Cool. Once cooled, polenta can be sliced and fried, baked or served with sauce.

Polenta lombarda

Lombardian polenta

6 servings

1 (10 ounce) package corn
  bread mix or
1 recipe Polenta, fried
4 tablespoons margarine or
  butter
2 (2–$2^1/_2$ pound) chickens,
  cut into 8 pieces
1 medium onion, chopped
1 (4 ounce) can sliced
  mushrooms
$^1/_4$ teaspoon dried sage
1 tablespoon flour
$^1/_4$ pound ham, diced
$^1/_2$ cup dry white wine

Prepare corn bread according to package directions or polenta according to recipe. Melt margarine in large skillet over medium heat. Brown chicken in margarine; remove. Add onion, mushrooms and sage to margarine; cook until onion is transparent. Add flour; stir until well blended. Add ham and chicken. Pour in wine. Cook over medium heat, stirring occasionally, about 25–30 minutes or until chicken is cooked. Serve over squares of corn bread or fried polenta.

Insalata saporita

Rice salad

4 servings

> 2 cups cold cooked rice
> $^1/_2$ cup cooked peas
> 4 ounces Swiss cheese, diced
> 1 ($1^3/_4$ ounce) can anchovy
>   fillets, chopped
> 1 (4 ounce) can Vienna
>   sausages, diced
> 4 lettuce leaves, optional
> 1 pimento, cut into strips
> $^1/_2$ yellow or green pepper, cut
>   into strips
> 3 gherkin pickles, sliced
>   Bottled Italian salad
>   dressing

Combine rice, peas, cheese, anchovies and Vienna sausages; toss lightly. Arrange on bed of lettuce. Garnish with pimento, pepper strips and pickle slices. Chill. Pour dressing over salad just before serving.

Gnocchi are eaten in Northern Italy. They are usually prepared with flour or semolina. Gnocchi dough is best when prepared just before serving.

Gnocchi verdi

Green dumplings

4 servings

- 1 (10 ounce) package frozen chopped spinach
- $^1/_2$ cup melted margarine or butter
- $^3/_4$ cup mashed potatoes
- 1 cup flour
- 1 cup fine bread crumbs
- 3 eggs, slightly beaten
- 1 teaspoon salt
- $^1/_8$ teaspoon nutmeg
- Dash black pepper
- $^1/_4$ cup grated Parmesan cheese
- Hot boiling water
- Tomato sauce

Cook and drain spinach well. Press through a fine sieve or blend smooth in blender. Combine spinach, $^1/_4$ cup margarine, potatoes, flour, bread crumbs, eggs, and seasonings; mix well. Divide dough into quarters. Shape each quarter into a roll 1″ in diameter. Cut roll into 1″ pieces. Repeat with remaining dough. Drop dough, a few pieces at a time into boiling water. Cook until dumplings come to surface. Remove; drain on paper towel. Place in shallow baking dish. Spoon remaining margarine over dumplings; sprinkle with grated cheese. Bake in a hot oven (400°) about 8 minutes. Serve with tomato sauce, if desired.

Gnocchi di semolino

Semolina dumplings

6 servings

- 2 cups milk
- $^3/_4$ cup farina
- 1 teaspoon salt
- Dash nutmeg
- 4 tablespoons melted margarine or butter
- 2 eggs, slightly beaten
- 6 tablespoons grated Parmesan cheese

Scald milk in heavy saucepan. Gradually add farina, salt, nutmeg and 2 tablespoons margarine, stirring constantly. Continue to cook, stirring constantly, until mixture is so thick that spoon stands up in it. Remove from heat. Beat in eggs and 2 tablespoons grated cheese. Spoon mixture into a shallow $15^1/_2″ \times 10^1/_2″ \times 1″$ greased jelly roll pan. Cool until firm. Cut semolina into circles with a $2^1/_2″$ cookie cutter. Place in 8″ baking dish. Dribble over remaining margarine; sprinkle with remaining cheese. Bake in a hot oven (400°) about 20 minutes or until golden brown.

Gnocchi di spinaci alla ricotta

Spinach and ricotta dumplings

6 servings

- 1 (10 ounce) package frozen chopped spinach
- $^3/_4$ pound Ricotta or cottage cheese
- 1 teaspoon salt
- 2 egg yolks
- 6 tablespoons grated Parmesan cheese
- 1 cup flour
- Hot water
- $^1/_4$ cup melted margarine or butter
- 1 teaspoon chopped parsley

Cook spinach and drain well. Combine spinach, Ricotta, salt, egg yolks, and 3 tablespoons Parmesan cheese. Drop mixture from a spoon into flour and shape into balls. Cook in large amount of simmering water about 5 minutes. Remove; drain on towel. Pour margarine over dumplings; sprinkle with remaining grated Parmesan cheese and parsley.

Pasta sauces

Salsa di pomodoro

Salsa bolognese

Salsa bruna all'italiana

Plain tomato sauce (1)

4 cups sauce

- 4 tablespoons olive oil
- 2 medium onions, chopped
- 1 clove garlic, minced
- 1/2 teaspoon dried basil
- 1/2 teaspoon salt
- 1/2 teaspoon sugar
  Dash black pepper
- 1 (29 ounce) can tomatoes
- 1 (6 ounce) can tomato paste

Heat oil in heavy saucepot; sauté onions and garlic in oil until onions are transparent. Stir in remaining ingredients. Cook over low heat, stirring frequently, until sauce thickens, about 40–45 minutes.

Plain tomato sauce (2)

4 cups sauce

- 3 tablespoons olive oil
- 3 cloves garlic, cut in half
- 4 (8 ounce) cans tomato sauce
- 1 (6 ounce) can tomato paste

Heat oil in heavy saucepot. Brown garlic in oil; remove. Stir in tomato sauce and paste. Cook over low heat, stirring frequently, until sauce thickens, about 30 minutes.

Bolognese sauce

4 cups sauce

- 3 tablespoons salad oil
- 1 medium onion, finely chopped
- 1 stalk celery, finely chopped
- 1 carrot, grated
- 1 clove garlic, minced
- 1/3 cup (2 ounce can) chopped mushrooms
- 1/2 pound ground beef
- 1/4 pound ham, ground
- 1/4 pound chicken livers, finely chopped
- 1 tablespoon flour
- 1/2 cup dry red wine
- 1 (8 ounce) can tomato sauce
- 1 teaspoon salt
- 1/2 teaspoon dried marjoram
- 1/2 teaspoon dried thyme
- 1/2 teaspoon sugar
- 1 bay leaf

Heat oil in large heavy saucepan; sauté onion, celery, carrot, garlic, and mushrooms in hot oil until onion is transparent. Add beef, ham and chicken livers; cook until meat is lightly browned. Spoon off excess fat. Stir in flour until well blended. Add wine; cook 3–5 minutes. Add remaining ingredients. Cook over medium heat, stirring occasionally, about 30 minutes. Press trough fine sieve or blend smooth in blender, if desired.

Brown sauce Italian style

4 cups sauce

- 2 tablespoons margarine or butter
- 1 large onion, finely chopped
- 1 clove garlic, minced
- 1 stalk celery, finely chopped
- 1 carrot, grated
- 1 (4 ounce) can chopped mushrooms
- 1 tablespoon parsley flakes
- 1/4 teaspoon thyme
- 1/4 pound ham, ground
- 1/2 cup dry red wine
- 3 tablespoons flour
- 1 (8 ounce) can tomato sauce
- 1 teaspoon salt
- 1/2 teaspoon sugar
- 3 cups water
- 3 beef bouillon cubes

Melt margarine in large heavy saucepan. Sauté onion, garlic, celery, carrot, mushrooms, parsley and thyme in margarine. Stir in ham; blend well; add wine. Heat flour in small skillet over low heat until flour turns brown; being careful not to burn. Stir flour into meat mixture; cook over low heat until mixture thickens, about 2–3 minutes. Add remaining ingredients; stir well. Cook uncovered over medium heat, stirring frequently, until sauce thickens, about 1 hour. Press through fine sieve or blend smooth in blender, if desired.

Salsa con carne e funghi

Meat and mushroom sauce

4 cups sauce

- 1 *pound lean ground beef*
- 1 *clove garlic, minced*
- 2 *(4 ounce) cans chopped mushrooms*
- $^1/_2$ *teaspoon dried basil*
- 2 *cups (28 ounce cans) tomato sauce*
- 1 *(6 ounce) can tomato paste*
- $^1/_2$ *teaspoon sugar*

Brown meat in heavy saucepan. Add remaining ingredients, stir well. Simmer uncovered, over medium heat, 30–35 minutes.

Egg dishes

Uova alla cacciatora

Eggs hunters' style

4 servings

- 4 tablespoons margarine or butter
- 2 tomatoes, thickly sliced
- 1 tablespoon chopped onion
- 4 chicken livers, cut into 4 pieces
- $\frac{1}{4}$ teaspoon salt
- $\frac{1}{8}$ teaspoon oregano
- 4 eggs
- 4 slices hot toast

Melt 2 tablespoons margarine in skillet; sauté tomatoes, turning once, until golden brown. Remove; keep warm. Cook onion and chicken livers in margarine until chicken livers are cooked; stir in salt, and oregano. In a separate skillet, melt remaining margarine. Break eggs gently into skillet. Gently cook eggs over low heat, spooning margarine over them 3–4 minutes or until of desired firmness. To serve, top each slice of toast with chicken livers, then with tomato slices and then egg.

The 'uova alla paesana', or fried eggs country style, are a delicious variation on bacon and eggs as we know it. They are a familiar farmer's breakfast from the Po valley in the North of Italy. Place a thick, tasty, golden-yellow slice of crispy bacon on the polenta, and crown with eggs fried sunny-side up, garnish with fried tomatoes, or serve with tomato sauce.

Uova fiorentina

Eggs Florentine

6 servings

- $^1/_4$ *cup margarine or butter*
- $^1/_4$ *cup flour*
- 1 *teaspoon salt*
- 2 *cups milk*
- 2 *(10 ounce) packages frozen chopped spinach*
- $^1/_4$ *teaspoon nutmeg*
- 12 *poached eggs*
- $^1/_4$ *cup grated Parmesan cheese*

Melt margarine in saucepan; blend in flour and salt. Gradually add milk, stirring constantly until well blended. Cook over medium heat, stirring constantly until thickened. Cook spinach; drain well. Combine $^1/_2$ cup white sauce and spinach; stir in nutmeg. Pour mixture into 6 ramikins or heat proof baking dishes. Arrange 2 eggs on top of each. Spoon remaining sauce over eggs. Sprinkle top with cheese. Bake in a hot oven (400°) until browned, about 10 minutes.

Uova affogate alla casalinga

Poached eggs on toast

4 servings

- 1 *(8 ounce) can tomato sauce*
- 4 *eggs*
- 2 *tablespoons margarine or butter*
- 1 *teaspoon anchovy paste*
- 4 *slices toast*
  Grated Parmesan cheese

Heat tomato sauce in skillet. Break eggs carefully into sauce; cover; poach over low heat about 5 minutes. Combine margarine and anchovy paste; blend well; spread on toast. Put one egg and some of the sauce over each slice of toast. Sprinkle with Parmesan cheese.

Uova e peperoni con salsicce

Eggs and pepper with sausages

4 servings

- 2 *tablespoons margarine or butter*
- 2 *tablespoons chopped onion*
- 4 *tablespoons chopped green pepper*
- 2 *tablespoons chopped pimento*
- $^1/_4$ *teaspoon oregano*
- 6 *eggs*
- 6 *tablespoons water*
- 6 *sweet Italian sausages, cooked*
- $^1/_2$ *cup tomato sauce, heated*

Melt margarine in large skillet over medium heat. Sauté onion, pepper, pimento and oregano until onion is transparent. Combine eggs and water; beat with a fork until light and foamy. Pour eggs into skillet. Cook slowly, gently lifting from bottom and sides with spoon as mixture sets, so liquid can flow to bottom. Do not stir. Cook until set but still moist. Arrange on serving platter with cooked sausages; spoon hot tomato sauce over eggs.

Frittata alla savoiarda

Savoy omelette

4 servings

- 4 *tablespoons margarine or butter*
- $^1/_2$ *cup diced ham*
- 1 *scallion, finely chopped*
- 1 *(4 ounce) can chopped mushrooms*
- 8 *eggs*
- 2 *tablespoons cold water*
- $^1/_2$ *teaspoon salt*
- $^1/_4$ *teaspoon dried basil*
- 2 *teaspoon parsley flakes*
- 2 *tablespoons grated Parmesan cheese*
- 4 *ounces mozzarella cheese, cubed*

Melt 2 tablespoons margarine in skillet; sauté ham, scallions and mushrooms. Melt remaining margarine in 10″ skillet or omelet pan. Tilt skillet back and forth to grease well. Combine eggs, water, salt, basil, parsley and 1 tablespoon Parmesan cheese; beat thoroughly with a fork until light and foamy. Pour egg mixture into skillet. As mixture sets at edge, with fork draw this portion toward center so uncooked portions flow to bottom. Shake skillet to keep omelet sliding free. Cook until eggs are still soft on top. Remove from heat. Spoon ham mixture over eggs; top with mozzarella cheese. Sprinkle with Parmesan cheese. Bake in a very hot oven (450°) just until cheese melts.

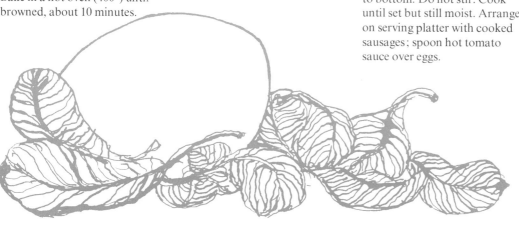

Fish dishes

For the 'zuppa di pesce'-recipe use as many different kinds of fish as possible

A visitor to an Italian fish market can see a harvest of sea food far richer than one could imagine. Fish from all over the Mediterranean lie on the stone slabs, their scales glittering in the bright sunshine, among them strange creatures that one would never have imagined could have come from the depths of such a beautiful, sparkling sea. Here are flashing blue and silver mackerel, elegantly flat sole, deep red mullet; there are monster-headed black rays, hideous John Dory's and squid with long purple fangs. Dark gray crabs crawl about in large boxes and lobsters, their claws bound, turn their untrusting beady eyes on passing shoppers. Mussels and other shellfish are piled in mounds. Adding to the color, the Italian merchants have decorated their counters with seaweed and bright yellow lemons.

Perhaps the most beautiful fishmarket in all Italy is the one in Venice. Imagine it early in the morning: there is a salty tang in the air as the fishing boats come through the mist, returning from their night on the Adriatic Sea to make their way up the Grand Canal to the market quay. The boats gently jostle against each other as they unload and the mist slowly rises revealing the ancient city.

Soon the market is full of housewives going from counter to counter inspecting the catch and selecting their purchases. Italian women are very choosy when it comes to buying; the poorer they are the more particular they are about what they buy. They carefully count each precious lira that they must spend. Right in the middle of the housewives are the cooks from the small trattorias and from the big restaurants. In Venice, even the chefs from the famous retaurants, such as the Gritti Palace, do their own shopping at the market. Choosing the ingredients is too important an affair to let someone else do the buying and they are determined that they will find the finest of the bright pink scampi and small rock lobsters which are among the most delicious in the world. You can eat these tasty shrimps in small or luxury restaurants in Venice and be sure of getting a delicacy. Scampi are the pride of Venice and from them each cook can prepare a meal fit for a king.

Zuppa di pesce

Fish soup

4 servings

- 1 pound fish fillets
- 2 cups water
- 2 tablespoons margarine or butter
- 1 small onion, chopped
- 1 clove garlic, minced
- 2 tablespoons chopped green pepper
- 1 stalk celery, chopped
- 2 medium potatoes, diced
- 1 (1 pound) can tomatoes
- 1 bay leaf
- 1 teaspoon salt
- $1/8$ teaspoon black pepper
- $1/4$ teaspoon dried oregano

Cut fish into serving pieces; place in saucepan. Add water. Cook over medium heat about 10 minutes or until fish flakes easily with a fork. Drain, reserving broth. Melt margarine in saucepot over medium heat. Sauté onion, garlic, pepper, and celery until onion is transparent. Stir in remaining ingredients and fish broth. Cook until potatoes are tender. Add fish; cook until heated throughout.

Zuppa di pesce alla genovese

Genoese fish soup

6 servings

- 1 pound fish fillets
- 4 cups water
- 2 tablespoons margarine or butter
- 1 medium onion, chopped
- 1 clove garlic, minced
- 1 (1 pound) can tomatoes
- 1 teaspoon dried sage
- $1/2$ teaspoon salt
  Dash black pepper
- $1/2$ pound shrimp, shelled and cleaned
- 2 tablespoons chopped parsley

Cut fish into bite-size pieces; place in saucepan. Add water. Cook over medium heat about 10 minutes or until fish flakes easily with a fork. Drain, reserving broth. Melt margarine in saucepot over medium heat. Sauté onion and garlic in margarine until onion is transparent. Stir in tomatoes, broth, sage, salt and pepper. Cook 3–5 minutes. Add shrimp and fish; cook just until shrimp turn pink. Garnish with parsley.

Zuppa di pesce alla napoletana

Neapolitan fish soup

6–8 servings

> 2 pounds fish fillets
> 6 cups water
> 4 tablespoons margarine or butter
> 2–3 cloves garlic, minced
> 3 tablespoons chopped parsley
> 1 cup dry white wine
> 2 tablespoons tomato paste
> 2 cups bottled clam juice
> 1 teaspoon salt
> 6 pounds assorted shellfish; lobster, crab, mussels, clams
> 1 tablespoon grated lemon peel
> Thick slices of Italian bread

Cut fish into serving size pieces; place in large saucepot. Add water. Cook over medium heat about 10 minutes or until fish flakes easily with a fork. Remove fish; keep broth hot. Melt margarine in large skillet; sauté garlic and 2 tablespoons parsley in margarine until lightly browned. Add wine, cook over high heat until reduced by half; stir in tomato paste, broth, clam juice and salt. Bring the soup to a rapid boil; add shellfish; boil rapidly 5 minutes. Add fish. Place fish and shellfish in serving dishes; ladle soup over fish; sprinkle with parsley and lemon peel. Serve with Italian bread.

Zuppa di baccalà

Cod fish soup

8 servings

> $1/4$ cup margarine or butter
> 3 medium onions, cut into rings
> 1 clove garlic, minced
> 1 stalk celery, chopped
> $1/2$ cup dry white wine, optional
> 3 medium tomatoes, chopped
> 1 carrot, sliced
> 2 large potatoes, cubed
> 1 tablespoon chopped parsley
> 1 bay leaf
> 1 teaspoon salt
> $1/8$ teaspoon black pepper
> 4 cups bottled clam juice
> $1^1/2$ pounds cod fish, cut into 2″ pieces

Melt margarine in large heavy saucepot. Sauté onions, garlic, and celery until onions are transparent. Stir in wine. Cook over high heat, stirring constantly, until wine is reduced by half. Add remaining ingredients. Cook over medium heat about 20–25 minutes or until fish is cooked.

Zuppa di vongole alla marinara

Sailor's clam soup

6 servings

> $1/4$ cup margarine or butter
> 1 medium onion, chopped
> 1 clove garlic, minced
> 1 cup dry white wine, optional
> 1 (16 ounce) can tomatoes
> 4 cups bottled clam juice
> 1 teaspoon salt
> $1/4$ teaspoon oregano
> Dash black pepper
> 2 cups clams, chopped
> 1 tablespoon chopped parsley

Melt margarine in saucepot. Sauté onion and garlic until onion is transparent. Stir in wine. Cook over high heat, stirring constantly until wine is reduced by half. Add tomatoes, clam juice, and seasonings; bring just to a boil. Add clams and parsley. Simmer 8–10 minutes.

Sgombro ripieno

Stuffed mackerel

4 servings

    2 tablespoons margarine or
       butter
    1 medium onion, finely
       chopped
    1 (4 ounce) can chopped
       mushrooms
    1 tablespoon parsley flakes
    1 teaspoon fennel seed,
       crushed
$^1/_2$ cup bread crumbs
$^1/_2$ teaspoon salt
    4 (1 pound) mackerel
    1 lemon, thinly sliced

Melt margarine in skillet over medium heat. Sauté onion, mushrooms, parsley and fennel seed in margarine until onion is transparent. Stir in bread crumbs and salt. Fill pocket of fish with stuffing; close opening with toothpicks. Place fish in shallow baking pan. Bake in a moderate oven (350°) about 15–20 minutes or until easily flaked with a fork. Garnish with lemon slices.

Anguille

Herbed eels

6 servings

  2 *pounds large eels*
  1 *cup flour*
  1 *tablespoon parsley flakes*
$^1/_2$ *teaspoon salt*
    Dash black pepper
  4 *tablespoons margarine or
    butter*
$^1/_2$ *cup dry white wine*
$^1/_2$ *cup water*
  1 *teaspoon lemon juice*
  2 *tablespoons parsley flakes*
  1 *tablespoon chopped chives*
$^1/_4$ *teaspoon salt*
$^1/_4$ *teaspoon dried mint*

Clean, skin and cut eels into
$2^1/_2''$ pieces. Combine flour, 1
tablespoon parsley, $^1/_2$ teaspoon
salt and pepper in large clean
brown paper bag. Drop eels in
bag, 2 or 3 pieces at a time;
shake until coated. (If there is
time let dry on rack 15–20
minutes). Melt margarine in
large skillet. Sauté eels in
margarine until lightly browned.
Add wine, water, lemon juice,
parsley, chives, salt and mint.
Cook over medium heat, about
10–15 minutes, basting eels
frequently.

Carpio arrosto

Baked carp

4 servings

$^1/_4$ *cup salad oil*
$^1/_4$ *cup dry white wine or
    vinegar*
  2 *tablespoons lemon juice*
  1 *tablespoon chopped parsley*
$^1/_4$ *teaspoon salt*
  4 *(1 pound) carp or perch
    fillets*
  1 *lemon, thinly sliced*

Combine oil, wine, lemon juice,
parsley and salt; pour over fish.
Cover; refrigerate 1 hour.
Remove fish from marinade;
place in $11^3/_4'' \times 7^1/_2'' \times 1^3/_4''$
baking dish. Bake in a moderate
oven (350°), basting frequently
with marinade, until fish are
done about 15–20 minutes.
Garnish with lemon slices.

Pesce alla paesana

Fish peasant style

4 servings

  2 *pounds fish fillets*
$^1/_4$ *teaspoon paprika*
  2 *tablespoons melted
    margarine or butter*
  1 *teaspoon fennel seed,
    crushed*
  1 *teaspoon parsley flakes*
$^1/_4$ *teaspoon dried thyme*
  1 *tablespoon lemon juice*
$^1/_2$ *cup dry white wine or*
$^1/_4$ *cup water*

Cut fish into serving pieces;
arrange in $11^3/_4'' \times 7^1/_2'' \times 1^3/_4''$
baking pan. Sprinkle fish with
paprika. Combine remaining
ingredients, pour over fish. Bake
in a moderate oven (375°) about
15–20 minutes or until fish
flakes easily with fork. Baste
frequently

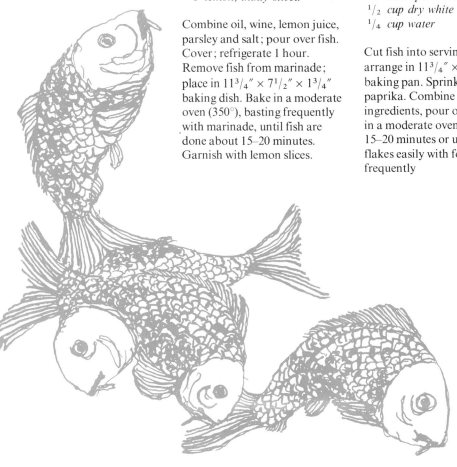

Filetti di pesce all'anice

Broiled fish fillets with anise

4 servings

$^1/_4$ *cup margarine or butter*
$^1/_4$ *teaspoon anise seed, crushed*
$^1/_2$ *cup dry white wine*
$^1/_8$ *teaspoon salt*
2 *pounds fish fillets*
1 *tablespoon chopped parsley*

Melt margarine in small skillet over medium heat, add anise seed; heat 1–2 minutes, stirring constantly. Add wine and salt; simmer 5–10 minutes. Cover broiler pan with aluminium foil; rub foil lightly with oil. Place fillets on foil; brush with margarine mixture. Broil 2″ from heat about 6–10 minutes. Do not turn. Place fish on serving platter; pour remaining sauce over fish. Garnish with chopped parsley.

Triglie alla livornese

Livornese Mullet

4 servings

4 *(8 ounces each) mullets*
2 *tablespoons margarine or butter*
1 *(1 pound) can tomatoes*
2 *strips lemon peel,* $^1/_4$″ *wide*
1 *bay leaf*

Clean and dry fish. Melt margarine in large skillet over medium heat. Sauté mullets in margarine, turning once, until lightly browned. Add remaining ingredients; cook over low heat, basting fish frequently, about 8–10 minutes or until fish flakes easily with a fork. Remove peel and bay leaf before serving.

Triglie alla graticola con finocchio

Mullet with fennel 'en papillote'

4 servings

$^3/_4$ *cup salad oil*
3 *tablespoons lemon juice*
4 *(8 ounces each) mullets, cleaned*
1 *large fennel bulb, thinly sliced or*
4 *stalks celery, thinly sliced*
1 *(6 ounce) package ham slices, cut in strips*
1 *teaspoon parsley flakes*
1 *lemon, thinly slices*

Combine oil and lemon juice; pour over fish. Cover; refrigerate 1 hour. Blanch fennel strips in boiling water about 1 minute; drain. Remove fish from marinade. Place 1 fish on large piece of foil; arrange fennel and ham strips on fish; sprinkle with parsley; top with 2 lemon slices. Close foil securely, using a drugstore wrap. Repeat with remaining ingredients. Bake in a moderate oven (350°) about 20–25 minutes.

Granchi

Crabmeat

2 servings

1 *(7 ounce) can crabmeat*
2 *tablespoons margarine or butter*
1 *lemon*
$^1/_8$ *teaspoon salt*
Dash black pepper
Hot cooked brown rice
1 *tablespoon chopped parsley*

Place crabmeat in 2 small ramikins or flame proof baking dishes. Dot with pats of margarine. Squeeze juice of half a lemon over each. Sprinkle with salt and pepper. Broil, 3″ from heat, until lightly browned and bubbly, about 4 minutes. Serve over hot rice. Garnish with chopped parsley.

Aragosta
Italians enjoy steamed or boiled
lobsters served with mayonnaise
or lemon butter

Fritto misto di pesce

Mixed fish-fry

6 servings

   1 *cup flour*
$^1/_4$ *teaspoon salt*
   3 *tablespoons salad oil*
$^3/_4$ *cup warm water*
   1 *egg white*
   1 *pound fish fillets*
 12 *shrimp, shelled and cleaned*
 12 *shucked clams*
     Oil or shortening for deep
     fat frying
     Lemon wedges

Combine flour and salt; stir in oil; mix well. Add water; blend well. If possible, let batter rest 2 hours, although it may be used at once. Beat egg white until stiff, but not dry; fold into batter. Cut fish fillets into bite-size pieces. Heat oil to 375°. Dip fish into batter; drop into fat. Deep-fry turning once, about 5–6 minutes or until golden brown. Remove from fat with tongs. Drain on absorbent paper; keep warm while remaining fish is fried. Garnish with lemon wedges.

Aragosta oreganata

Lobster oregano

2 servings

- 2 (1$^1/_2$–2 pounds) lobsters
- $^1/_2$ cup melted margarine or butter
- $^1/_2$ cup seasoned bread crumbs
- 2 tablespoons grated Parmesan cheese
- 1 teaspoon grated onion

Split and clean lobster; crack claws. Place lobster, meat side up on broiler rack, 4″ from heat. Brush well with margarine. Broil 10–12 minutes, brushing with margarine now and then. Combine bread crumbs, cheese and onion. Sprinkle lobster with crumb mixture. Pour remaining margarine over crumbs; broil 5 minutes longer. Garnish with lemon wedges and parsley, if desired.

Aragosta alla marsala

Lobster in wine

2 servings

- 2 (1$^1/_2$–2 pound) lobsters
- 3 tablespoons oil or margarine
- 1 small onion, finely chopped
- 1 small clove garlic, cut in half
- 1 cup dry white wine
- 2 tomatoes, quartered and seeded
- 1 tablespoon parsley flakes
- $^1/_2$ teaspoon dried oregano
- $^1/_2$ teaspoon salt
- Dash cayenne pepper

Split lobster in half lengthwise; remove stomach sacks and intestinal tubes. Remove and crack claws and joints. Separate tails from chests. Heat oil or margarine in large skillet. Add lobster pieces, meat-side down; sauté for several minutes, turning with tongs, until shells are bright red. Remove lobster and keep warm. Sauté onion and garlic in skillet. Add remaining ingredients. Bring mixture to a boil; cook until liquid is reduced by half. Add lobster; simmer 8–10 minutes, basting every few minutes. Arrange lobster pieces on a warm platter and spoon sauce over them. Garnish with watercress and lemon wedges, if desired.

Passera con peperoni

Flounder with peppers

6 servings

- 4 tablespoons margarine or butter
- 2 medium onions, sliced
- 1 green pepper, cut into rings
- 1 red pepper, cut into rings
- 1 cup dry white wine
- $^3/_4$ teaspoon chervil
- $^1/_4$ teaspoon salt
- Dash black pepper
- 2 pounds flounder fillets

Melt margarine in large skillet. Sauté onions and peppers just until onions are transparent. Stir in wine, chervil, salt and pepper. Simmer 5 minutes. Place fish fillets in buttered 11$^3/_4$″ × 7$^1/_2$″ × 1$^3/_4$″ baking dish; pour onion mixture over fish. Bake, basting frequently, in a moderate oven (350°) about 25–30 minutes or until fish flakes easily when tested with a fork.

Merluzzo con erbe

Haddock with herbs

6 servings

- 2 pounds haddock fillets
- 1 (1 pound) can tomatoes
- 1 clove garlic, minced
- 1 tablespoon salad oil
- 1 teaspoon parsley flakes
- $^1/_4$ teaspoon dried oregano
- $^1/_4$ teaspoon dried thyme

Place fish in buttered 11$^3/_4$″ × 7$^1/_2$″ × 1$^3/_4$″ baking dish. Combine remaining ingredients; pour over fish. Bake, basting frequently, in a moderate oven (350°) about 25–30 minutes or until fish flakes easily when tested with a fork.

Trotelle con finocchio

Trout with fennel

4 servings

> 2 *fennel bulbs*
> 1 *quart boiling water*
> 1 *tablespoon lemon juice*
> 4 *brook trout, cleaned*
> 1 *cup dry white wine*
> $^1/_4$ *teaspoon salt*
> 1 *bay leaf*

Wash fennel; cut into $^1/_2$" strips. Cook fennel in boiling water 2–3 minutes; drain well. Place fennel in buttered 11$^3/_4$" × 7$^1/_2$" × 1$^3/_4$" baking dish; sprinkle with lemon juice. Place fish on fennel. Pour wine over fish; sprinkle with salt; add bay leaf. Bake in a moderate oven (350°) 20–25 minutes; baste frequently. Remove from oven; keep fish warm. Drain liquid from baking dish; bring to a boil; cook until liquid is reduced to 1 cup. Pour over fish before serving.

Calamaretti ripieni al forno

Baked stuffed squid

4 servings

> 2 *(1 pound each) squid,*
>   *cleaned and skinned*
> $^1/_2$ *cup melted margarine*
>   *or butter*
> 2 *cups soft bread crumbs*
> 1 *tablespoon onion flakes*
> $^1/_4$ *teaspoon salt*
> $^1/_4$ *teaspoon dried thyme*
>   *Dash black pepper*
> 1 *(1 pound can) tomatoes*
> 1 *cup dry white wine,*
>   *optional*

Chop squid tenticles. Combine tenticles, margarine, bread crumbs, onion, salt, thyme and pepper; toss lightly to mix. Stuff squid with bread mixture. Close opening with toothpicks. Place in 11$^3/_4$" × 7$^1/_2$" × 1$^3/_4$" baking dish. Pour tomatoes and wine over squid. Bake in a moderate oven (350°) about 35–40 minutes, basting frequently.

Filetti di sogliola alla fiorentina

Fillet of sole Florentine style

6 servings

> 1 *cup dry white wine*
> $^1/_2$ *cup fish stock or water*
> 2 *pounds fillet of sole*
> 3 *tablespoons margarine*
>   *or butter*
> 2 *tablespoons flour*
> $^1/_2$ *teaspoon salt*
> 1 *(10 ounce) package*
>   *frozen chopped spinach*
> $^1/_4$ *cup grated Parmesan*
>   *cheese*

Combine wine and fish stock in large skillet; bring to a boil. Lower heat; add the sole; poach fish gently about 10 minutes or until fish flakes easily when tested with a fork. Remove fish; keep warm. Boil liquid until reduced to 1 cup. Melt 2 tablespoons margarine in small skillet; stir in flour and salt until well blended. Gradually stir in reduced wine mixture. Cook over medium heat, stirring constantly, until thickened. Cook spinach; drain well; stir in remaining margarine. Place spinach in buttered 11$^3/_4$" × 7$^1/_2$" × 1$^3/_4$" baking dish. Arrange fish fillets on spinach; pour sauce over fish. Sprinkle with grated Parmesan cheese. Bake in a very hot oven (425°) until cheese is browned.

Code di scampi fritte

Shrimp and zucchini

4 servings

> 4 *tablespoons margarine*
>   *or butter*
> 20 *large schrimp, shelled*
>   *and cleaned*
> 2 *medium zucchini, sliced*
> 1 *tablespoon lemon juice*
> $^1/_4$ *teaspoon salt*
>   *Dash black pepper*
> 1 *scallion, chopped*

Melt margarine in large skillet over medium heat. Add shrimp and zucchini; cook, stirring constantly, until shrimp are pink and tender, about 5–8 minutes. Stir in lemon juice, salt and pepper. Garnish with chopped scallion.

Gamberi con riso

Shrimp and rice

4 servings

     4 tablespoons margarine
        or butter
     1 medium onion, chopped
 $^1/_4$ cup finely chopped celery
     1 (1 pound) can tomatoes
 $^1/_2$ teaspoon dried basil
 $^1/_2$ teaspoon salt
        Dash black pepper
    20 large shrimp, shelled
        and cleaned
     1 (10 ounce) package
        frozen peas
        Hot cooked rice

Melt margarine in skillet; sauté
onion and celery in margarine
until onion is transparent. Stir
in tomatoes, basil, salt and
pepper; bring to a boil. Reduce
heat; add shrimp and peas.
Cook over low heat until shrimp
are pink and tender, about 8–10
minutes. Serve over hot rice.

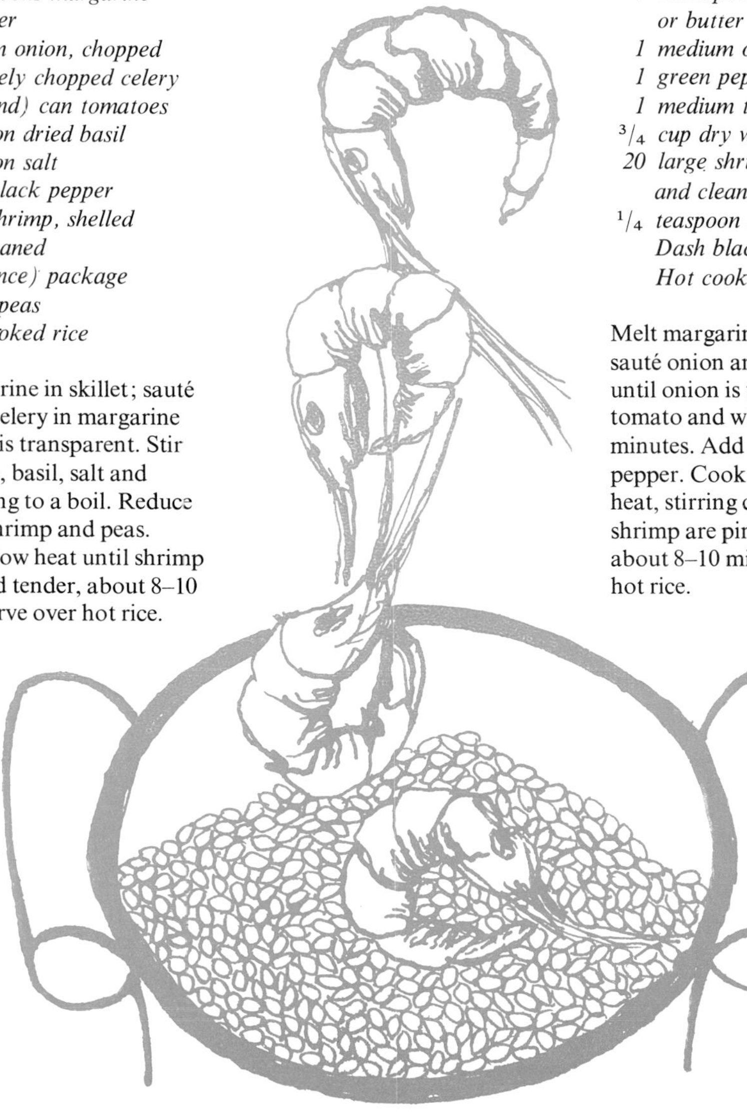

Gamberi alla mario

Shrimp Mario

4 servings

     4 tablespoons margarine
        or butter
     1 medium onion, sliced
     1 green pepper, chopped
     1 medium tomato, quartered
 $^3/_4$ cup dry white wine
    20 large shrimp, shelled
        and cleaned
 $^1/_4$ teaspoon salt
        Dash black pepper
        Hot cooked rice

Melt margarine in large skillet;
sauté onion and green pepper
until onion is transparent. Add
tomato and wine; cook 3–5
minutes. Add shrimp, salt and
pepper. Cook over medium
heat, stirring constantly, until
shrimp are pink and tender,
about 8–10 minutes. Serve over
hot rice.

Vongole alla siciliana

Steamed clams Siciliana

4 servings

    24 hard shell clams
     2 tablespoons salad oil
     2 cloves garlic, minced
 $^1/_4$ cup dry white wine
 $^1/_4$ cup water
     1 tablespoon parsley
        flakes
 $^1/_4$ teaspoon salt
        Dash black pepper
        Lemon wedges

Scrub clams under running
water until free of sand. Heat oil
in large saucepot; sauté garlic in
hot oil. Stir in remaining
ingredients. Place clams in
saucepot. Cover; steam until
shells just open. Heap clams in
soup dish. Spoon sauce over
clams, Garnish with lemon
wedges.

Pesce alla griglia

Grilled fish

Many fish are excellent for broiling, either indoors or out. Whole fish, fish steaks and even fillets can be broiled successfully with a little care.

When broiling in the range remember to follow the manufacturers directions. Always oil the broiler pan or lay a sheet of foil over it. Broil fish 3–4″ from heat. Whole fish and fish steaks should be turned once during cooking. Do not turn fillets. Brush fish well with melted margarine or oil; fillets need more lubrication than whole fish or fish steaks. Broil fillets 5–10 minutes, depending on thickness. Steaks will take from 6–12 minutes and whole fish 10–20 minutes, depending on size. *Do not overcook*. Fish is done when it flakes easily when tested with a fork.

To charcoal broil. Place fish in a greased hinged grill as it will be easier to turn. Make sure coals are white hot. Turn fish once or twice during cooking. A whole fish will take about 8 minutes each side. while fish fillets take only $1^1/_2$–2 minutes per side.

Serve broiled fish plain with lemon, or with lemon butter, parsley butter or your favorite herb butter.

Bistecca fiorentina

Florentine steak

6 servings

4 tablespoons parsley
 flakes
1 teaspoon dried oregano
1 teaspoon dried basil
$^1/_4$ teaspoon dried thyme
4 tablespoons salad oil
1 (2″ thick) round steak
$1^1/_2$ teaspoon salt
$^1/_2$ teaspoon garlic salt
 Freshly ground black
 pepper
$^1/_2$ cup dry red wine
6 large mushrooms caps
2 tablespoons melted
 margarine or butter
12 rolled anchovy fillets

Combine parsley, oregano, basil and thyme; mix well. Place steak on large piece heavy duty foil. Rub 2 tablespoons oil on 1 side of steak; sprinkle with half the salt, garlic salt and plenty of black pepper. Sprinkle half the herb mixture over steak; gently pat herbs into steak. Turn steak over; use remaining oil, salt, garlic salt, pepper and herb mixture. Pour wine on steak. Close foil securely, using a drug store wrap. Let steak marinate in foil, 3–4 hours, turning once or twice. If steak is to be marinated longer than 4 hours, refrigerate. Broil steak in foil, 3–4″ from heat, 10 minutes each side. Remove foil. Brush mushroom caps with melted margarine; place on broiler pan with steak. Continue to broil 3–4 minutes, each side of steak, or until desired doneness. Slice steak diagonally to serve. Garnish with broiled mushroom caps and rolled anchovy fillets.

Bolliti misti

Mixed boiled meat

8 servings

Meat:
2 pounds bottom round,
  in 1 piece
1 pound boneless veal
10 Italian sweet or hot
  sausages
1 onion
1 clove garlic, minced
2 carrots, chopped
1 leek, chopped
1 tablespoon salt
$^1/_4$ teaspoon dried thyme
$^1/_4$ teaspoon dried marjoram
1 ($2^1/_2$–3 pound) chicken,
  cut into 8 pieces

Vegetables:
2 pounds small white
  onions, peeled
12 carrots, cut into quarters
1 large turnip, cubed
8 small potatoes, peeled
8 small leeks, cleaned

Green sauce:
1 cup parsley, chopped
4 anchovy fillets
2 tablespoons capers
1 clove garlic, cut in half
1 onion, quartered
1 cup olive oil
2 tablespoons lemon juice

Combine bottom round, veal,
sausages, onion, garlic, carrots,
leek, salt, thyme and marjoram
in large saucepot. Cover with
water. Bring to a boil; reduce
heat; simmer $1^1/_2$ hours. Skim
off foam. Add chicken; simmer

30–35 minutes.
Thirty minutes before meat has
finished cooking, add onions,
carrots, turnip and potatoes to
boiling salted water in large
saucepot. Cook, uncovered, 10
minutes. Add leeks, cook 20–25
minutes longer.
Place all ingredients for the
green sauce in blender; blend
until smooth.
When ready to serve, arrange
meat and vegetables in a large
deep platter or serving dish.
Spoon some of the hot meat
broth over all. Serve with green
sauce.

Polpette

Meatballs

6 servings

1 pound ground beef
$^1/_2$ pound ground pork
2 eggs
$^1/_4$ cup bread crumbs
3 tablespoons parsley flakes
1 teaspoon salt
1 teaspoon grated lemon
  rind
$^1/_4$ teaspoon dried oregano
$^1/_4$ teaspoon black pepper
1 tablespoon salad oil

Combine all ingredients except
oil; mix lightly to blend. Shape
into 12 balls. Heat oil in large
skillet; brown meatballs in oil
until cooked to desired doneness.

Skewers

1 recipe for meatballs
$^1/_2$ pound salami, cut
  into 1" cubes
1 green pepper
12 small canned onions
2 tablespoons melted
  margarine or butter

Prepare meatball recipe as
above. Shape into 24 rolls 2"
long and 1" wide. Blanch and
seed pepper; cut into 1" chunks.
Thread meatballs, pepper,
salami and onions alternately on
skewers. Brush vegetables with
margarine. Broil, 3–4" from
heat, until meatballs are cooked,
about 5 minutes, turning
frequently.

Stufatino di bue alla romana

Roman beef stew

8 servings

6 slices bacon, diced
3 pounds beef for stew,
  cut into $1^1/_2$" cubes
1 onion, sliced
1 clove garlic, minced
$^1/_2$ cup dry red wine
1 (29 ounce) can tomatoes
1 teaspoon salt
$^1/_2$ teaspoon dried marjoram
$^1/_4$ teaspoon black pepper
6 large carrots, cut
  into 2" pieces
1 pound small whole
  onions, peeled
4 medium potatoes,
  quartered
$^1/_2$ pound zucchini, sliced
2 tablespoons flour, optional

Cook bacon until crisp in large
Dutch oven. Remove bacon;
pour off drippings, returning 3
tablespoons to pot. Brown meat
in drippings, turning often. Add
onion, garlic, wine, tomatoes,
marjoram, salt and pepper.
Cover. Simmer $1^1/_2$ hours,
stirring occasionally. Add
carrots, onions and potatoes.
Cover. Cook 35–40 minutes or
until vegetables are tender. Add
zucchini, and bacon; cook 10
minutes or until zucchini is
tender. Thicken liquid with 2
tablespoons flour if desired.

Bistecca con peperoni e pomodori

Steak with peppers and tomatoes

4 servings

> 4 tablespoons margarine
>   or butter
> $1^1/_2$ pounds sirloin steak,
>   cut into 1" cubes
> 2 green peppers, cut
>   into strips
> 2 tomatoes, chopped
> 1 teaspoon dried oregano
> 1 teaspoon Worcestershire
>   sauce
> $^1/_2$ teaspoon salt
> $^1/_8$ teaspoon black pepper
>   Italian bread, cut
>   into 1" slices

Melt margarine in large skillet over medium heat. Brown meat in margarine; remove; keep warm. Add peppers, tomatoes, oregano, Worcestershire sauce, salt and pepper. Cook 5 minutes or until peppers are softened. Return meat. Cook 2–3 minutes or until steak is of desired doneness. Serve over sliced bread.

Casseruole di manza e melanzane

Beef and eggplant casserole

8–10 servings

> 2 pounds ground beef
> 1 medium onion, chopped
> 1 green pepper, chopped
> 2 (8 ounce) cans tomato
>   sauce
> 1 teaspoon salt
> $^1/_2$ teaspoon dried oregano
> $^1/_2$ teaspoon dried basil
> $^1/_8$ teaspoon black pepper
> 2 medium eggplants,
>   cut into 2" cubes
> $^1/_2$ pound mozzarella
>   cheese, sliced

Brown meat in heavy skillet. Add onion and pepper; cook about 2 minutes, stirring frequently. Add tomato sauce, salt, oregano, basil, and pepper; stir well to blend. Cook 5–10 minutes. Place eggplant in buttered $13^3/_4$" × $9^1/_2$" × 2" baking dish. Pour meat mixture over eggplant. Bake in a moderate oven (350°) about 20–25 minutes or until hot and bubbly. Arrange cheese slices on meat. Continue to bake 5–10 minutes or until cheese melts.

Medaglione di vitello alla piemontese

Veal cutlets Piedmont style

4 servings

> 4 tablespoons margarine
>   or butter
> 4 veal cutlets, $^1/_2$" thick
> $^1/_2$ cup dry white wine
> $^1/_2$ teaspoon salt
> $^1/_4$ teaspoon dried basil
> $^1/_8$ teaspoon black pepper
> 4 slices provolone
>   cheese

Melt margarine in large skillet. Brown veal cutlets in margarine. Add wine, salt, basil and pepper. Cook over low heat, basting frequently, 10–12 minutes. Place cutlets in shallow baking dish. Pour wine sauce over veal. Place 1 slice of cheese over each cutlet. Bake in a hot oven (400°) about 10 minutes or until cheese is melted.

Scaloppine di vitello al marsala

Veal scallops in Marsala wine

4 servings

> 12 thin veal cutlets
> $^1/_2$ teaspoon salt
>   Dash black pepper
> $^1/_4$ cup flour
> 4 tablespoons margarine
>   or butter
> $^1/_2$ cup Marsala wine
> $^1/_4$ cup beef bouillon

Flatten veal cutlets between sheets of plastic wrap with smooth mallet. Sprinkle with salt, pepper and flour; shake off excess flour. Melt margarine in large skillet. Brown veal on both sides in margarine; remove; keep warm. Stir wine into pan juices. Mix 1 tablespoon of the flour used for dredging with the bouillon. Add to skillet; cook over medium heat until thickened, stirring constantly. Pour over cutlets. Serve with stewed tomatoes, if desired.

This dish is traditionally served with 'risotto milanese' (recipe on page no. 38) but it can also be served with a spaghetti or other pasta dish.

Ossobucco alla milanese

Scaloppine

Ossobucco alla milanese

Veal shanks Milanese style

6 servings

>   6 veal shanks, about
>   2$^1/_2$" thick
> $^1/_2$ cup flour
> $^1/_2$ cup salad oil
>   1 onion, finely chopped
>   1 carrot, grated
>   1 stalk celery, finely
>   chopped
>   2 cloves garlic, minced
>   1 teaspoon dried marjoram
> $^1/_2$ cup dry white wine,
>   optional
>   1 (1 pound) can tomatoes
>   1 cup beef bouillon
>   1 tablespoon chopped
>   parsley
>   1 teaspoon grated lemon
>   rind

Dredge veal shanks with flour. Heat oil in large Dutch oven. Brown veal in hot oil; remove. Add onion, carrot, celery, 1 clove garlic and marjoram. Cook over medium heat, stirring constantly, about 3 minutes. Add wine, cook until wine is reduced by half. Return veal shanks; add tomatoes and bouillon. Cover. Simmer 1–1$^1/_2$ hours or until veal is tender. Stir in remaining garlic, parsley and lemon rind; cook 1 minute.

Braciuolini di vitello

Veal rollettes

6–8 servings

>   1 (1$^3/_4$ ounce) can
>   anchovy fillets, optional
> $^1/_4$ cup milk
>   8 veal cutlets, $^1/_8$" thick
>   8 slices prosciutto or ham
>   8 slices provolone cheese
>   4 tablespoons margarine
>   or butter
>   1 tablespoon chopped parsley
>   1 tablespoon lemon juice

Soak anchovies in milk, 15 minutes, to remove excess salt; rinse; dry on paper towel. On each slice of veal place 1 slice of prosciutto, 1 slice of cheese, and 2 anchovies. Roll and fasten securely with toothpicks. Melt margarine in large skillet. Brown veal rolls on all sides in margarine. Stir in parsley and lemon juice. Cook over medium heat, basting rolls frequently, until veal is cooked, about 12–15 minutes.

Cosciotto d'agnello all'abruzzese

Leg of lamb from the Abruzzi

10–12 servings

1–2 cloves garlic, optional
*1 (6–8 pound) leg of
    lamb, well trimmed*
*1 (1 pound) can
    tomatoes, drained*
$^1/_2$ cup dry red wine
1 tablespoon parsley flakes
1 teaspoon salt
*$^1/_2$ teaspoon dried
    rosemary, crushed*
$^1/_8$ teaspoon black pepper

Cut garlic into thin slivers. Cut small slits in lamb and insert garlic. Place meat in roasting bag, which has been dusted with flour. Combine remaining ingredients; pour over meat in bag. Tie bag securely. Puncture 6 holes in top of bag. Place bag in roasting pan. Roast in a slow oven (325°) about 2$^1/_2$–3 hours or until cooked to desired degree of doneness.

Agnello brodettato

Lamb chops with lemon sauce

6 servings

2 tablespoons salad oil
*6 (1" thick) shoulder
    lamb chops*
1 clove garlic, minced
1 tablespoon parsley flakes
$^1/_2$ cup dry white wine
$^1/_2$ cup water
3 egg yolks
2 tablespoons lemon juice

Heat oil in large skillet. Brown chops well in hot oil. Add garlic, parsley, wine and water. Cook over medium heat, about 15 minutes or until chops are tender. Remove chops; keep warm. Cook liquid until reduced by half. Beat egg yolks slightly; add lemon juice. Stir a small amount of hot skillet mixture into eggs; return to skillet. Cook over low heat, stirring constantly until slightly thickened. Pour over lamb chops before serving.

Agnello allo spiedino

Lamb skewers

6 servings

*1$^1/_2$ pounds boneless lamb,
    cut into 1" pieces*
*1 (8 ounce) bottle Italian
    salad dressing*
*2 small zucchini, cut
    into 1" slices*
12 cherry tomatoes
*2 tablespoons melted
    margarine or butter*

Place lamb in bowl; pour salad dressing over meat; toss lightly to coat meat. Let stand 4 hours. If meat is to be marinated more than 4 hours, refrigerate. Cook zucchini in boiling salted water 3–4 minutes; drain. Thread meat, tomatoes and zucchini alternately on skewers. Brush tomatoes and zucchini with melted margarine. Broil 4–5" from heat, turning frequently, about 10–12 minutes or until done.

Agnello alla romana

Roast young leg of lamb Roman style

6–8 servings

1 cup fine bread crumbs
$^1/_2$ cup finely chopped parsley
2 cloves garlic, minced
1 teaspoon salt
$^1/_8$ teaspoon black pepper
1 (5–6 pound) leg of lamb
4 tablespoons olive oil

Combine bread crumbs, parsley, garlic, salt and pepper; mix well. Place lamb in large open roasting pan; brush with two tablespoons oil. Coat entire leg of lamb with crumb mixture. Drizzle remaining oil over surface. Insert meat thermometer. Roast in a moderate oven (350°) until meat thermometer registers 165° for medium or 175° for well-done, about 2–2$^1/_2$ hours. Serve hot.

Mixed boiled meat

Agnello in umido con zucchini

Lamb stew with zucchini

4–6 servings

> 2 *tablespoons salad oil*
> 2 *pounds boneless lean*
>   *lamb cubes*
> 1 *medium onion, chopped*
> 1 *(8 ounce) can tomato sauce*
> $^1/_4$ *cup dry white wine*
> 1 *teaspoon dried oregano*
> $^1/_2$ *teaspoon salt*
>   *Dash black pepper*
> $1^1/_4$ *pounds zucchini or*
>   *yellow summer squash,*
>   *sliced*

Heat oil in large skillet; brown lamb in oil over medium heat. Add onions; cook, stirring constantly, about 1 minute. Stir in tomato sauce, wine, oregano, salt and pepper. Cover. Simmer until tender, about 45 minutes. Add water if needed. Add zucchini; cook until tender, about 10 minutes. Serve hot.

Prosciutto all'italiana

Glazed baked ham

8–10 servings

> 1 *(5 pound) boneless ham*
> 2 *cups Marsala wine*
> 1 *cup brown sugar*
> 1 *tablespoon prepared*
>   *mustard*

Place ham in roasting pan; pour wine into pan. Cover. Roast in a moderate oven (350°) about $1^1/_2$ hours; baste occasionally with wine. Remove from oven. Meanwhile, mix sugar and mustard together to make a thick paste. Score top of ham; spread with sugar mixture. Return to oven. Increase temperature to 425°. Bake 20 minutes or until glaze forms on top of ham. Remove ham from oven; let stand 10–15 minutes before carving.

Costolette di maiale alla modenese

Modenese pork chops

4 servings

> 4 *tablespoons margarine*
>   *or butter*
> 4 *loin pork chops,*
>   *about 1″ thick*
> $^1/_2$ *cup dry white wine*
> 1 *teaspoon salt*
> $^1/_8$ *teaspoon black pepper*
> 1 *teaspoon dried sage,*
>   *crushed*
> 1 *teaspoon dried*
>   *rosemary, crushed*
> 2 *cloves garlic, minced*
> 2 *tablespoons lemon juice*

Melt margarine in large skillet over medium heat. Brown chops on each side in margarine. Add wine, salt, pepper, sage, rosemary and garlic. Cover. Simmer about 20 minutes, until chops are tender, turning once during cooking. Remove chops to warm platter. Add lemon juice to pan juices. Simmer 1 minute. Pour over chops and serve.

Cazzuola di maiale alla milanese

Milanese pork stew

6 servings

> 6 *sweet Italian sausages*
> $2^1/_2$ *pounds pork shoulder*
>   *meat, cut into 1″ cubes*
> 4 *tablespoons olive oil*
> 1 *medium onion, chopped*
> 1 *clove garlic, minced*
> $^1/_4$ *pound salt pork,*
>   *thinly sliced*
> 1 *cup water*
> 1 *teaspoon salt*
> $^1/_4$ *teaspoon black pepper*
> 2 *small cabbages, cut*
>   *into quarters*

Prick sausages with fork; brown in large heavy skillet. Remove from skillet; keep warm. Heat oil; brown pork cubes in olive oil; remove. Cook onion and garlic in oil until onion is transparent. Add salt pork; cook until crisp. Stir in pork cubes, water, salt, and pepper. Cover. Simmer about $1^1/_2$ hours, or until pork is tender and thoroughly cooked. Add cabbage quarters; top with browned sausages. Cover. Cook until cabbage is tender and sausages are completely heated, about 20–25 minutes.

Arrosto di maiale

Roast pork

8 servings

> 1 (6–7 pound) loin of pork
> 1 teaspoon salt
> 1/4 teaspoon black pepper
> 1/2 teaspoon caraway seed
> 1 teaspoon dried rosemary
> 2–3 cloves garlic, cut into slivers
> 2 green apples, peeled and sliced
> 1 orange, peeled and sliced

Rub loin of pork with salt, pepper, caraway seed, and rosemary. Make slits in meat and insert slivers of garlic. Dust inside of roasting bag with flour. Place meat in bag; arrange apple and orange slices on top of meat. Close bag with fastener; cut 4–5 slits in top of bag with knife, following manufacturer's directions. Place in shallow roasting pan. Bake in slow oven (325°) until done, about $2^1/_2$–3 hours. Slit top of roasting bag carefully; remove roast. Remove garlic from meat. Garnish with fresh orange slices.

Casseruola di legumi e salsicce

Vegetable and sausage casserole

6 servings

> 1 large eggplant, peeled and cubed
> 1 medium zucchini, sliced
> 1 green pepper, cut into strips
> 2 medium onions, sliced
> 1 teaspoon dried oregano
> 1/2 teaspoon salt
> 1 (16 ounce) jar marinara sauce
> $1^1/_4$ pound Italian sausages
> 1/2 pound mozzarella cheese, sliced
> 1/2 pound provolone cheese, sliced

Place alternate layers of half the eggplant, zucchini, pepper and onions in $2^1/_2$-quart casserole. Repeat. Sprinkle with oregano and salt. Pour sauce over vegetables. Cover. Bake in a moderate oven (375°), 45 minutes. Place sausages in shallow baking dish; prick sausages with fork. During the last 30 minutes bake in oven with vegetable casserole, Remove casserole and sausages from oven. Drain sausages. Place on top of vegetables. Arrange mozzarella over sausages; provolone slices over mozzarella. Return to oven. Bake 5–10 minutes or until cheese melts.

Salsicce con fagioli stufati in umido

Sausage and beans

6 servings

> 1 pound Italian sausage
> 1 clove garlic, minced
> 2 medium onions, chopped
> 1/2 cup chopped celery
> 1/2 teaspoon dried rosemary
> 1/2 teaspoon salt
> 1/4 teaspoon black pepper
> 1 can (20 ounce) white kidney beans
> 1 can (16 ounces) tomatoes

Brown sausage in large skillet; remove; keep warm. Pour off drippings, returning 2 tablespoons to skillet. Sauté garlic, onions, and celery until onions are transparent; add rosemary, salt, and pepper. Stir in beans, tomatoes, and sausage. Simmer about 8–10 minutes. Serve immediately.

Fegato con vino

Liver and wine

4 servings

> 4 slices (about $1^1/_2$ pounds) beef liver
> 1 teaspoon dried marjoram
> 1/2 teaspoon salt
> Dash black pepper
> 1/4 cup flour
> 1/3 cup olive oil
> 2 medium onions, sliced
> 1/2 cup dry red wine
> 1/4 cup orange juice
> Orange slices

Sprinkle both sides of liver slices with marjoram, salt, pepper and flour; shake off excess flour. Heat oil in large skillet. Sauté onions in hot oil over medium heat until transparent. Remove onions; drain on paper towel. Fry liver slices 4–5 minutes, turning once. Place liver on warm platter; keep warm. Stir one tablespoon of the flour used for dredging into orange juice. Add to skillet; stir in wine and onions. Cook over medium heat, stirring constantly, until thickened. Pour over liver. Garnish with orange slices.

Game and fowl dishes

Pollo alla cacciatora

Chicken hunters' style

4 servings

- 4 tablespoons salad oil
- 1 (3 pound) chicken, cut into 8 pieces
- 2 thick slices bacon, diced
- 2 medium onions, chopped
- 1 ($4^1/_2$ ounce) can sliced mushrooms, drained
- 1 tablespoon chopped parsley
- 1 teaspoon dried basil
- 1 teaspoon salt
- $^1/_8$ teaspoon black pepper
- $^1/_4$ cup dry white wine
- 1 (1 pound) can tomatoes, drained
- 1 (10 ounce) package frozen peas, cooked

Heat oil in large skillet; brown chicken; remove. Add bacon; cook about 1 minute over medium heat. Add onions and mushrooms; cook until onions are transparent. Return chicken to skillet; sprinkle with parsley, basil, salt and pepper. Add wine and tomatoes. Cover. Simmer, turning once, until tender about 25–30 minutes. Remove chicken to heated platter; pour sauce over chicken. Arrange peas around chicken. Serve at once.

Pollo imbottito arrostito

Roast chicken with ham stuffing

6 servings

- 1 *(4–5 pound) roasting chicken*
- 3 *tablespoons olive oil*
- 4 *bread slices, cubed*
- 1 *egg*
- 4 *ounces prosciutto or smoked ham, chopped*
- 1 *tablespoon chopped parsley*
- 1 *clove garlic, minced*
- $^1/_2$ *teaspoon salt*
- $^1/_4$ *teaspoon dried marjoram*
- $^1/_8$ *teaspoon black pepper*
- $^1/_4$ –$^1/_2$ *cup chicken bouillon*

Rub chicken with olive oil inside and out. Combine remaining ingredients; mix lightly. Stuff body and neck cavities of chicken lightly; truss. Place chicken on rack in roasting pan. Roast in a slow oven (325°) $1^1/_2$–2 hours or until chicken is tender and well browned. Remove chicken from oven. Place on serving platter. Remove stuffing from chicken; arrange around chicken. Garnish with quartered tomato.

Filetti di pollo alla bolognese

Bolognese breast of chicken

4 servings

- 2 *whole boned chicken breasts*
- $^1/_2$ *teaspoon salt*
  Dash black pepper
- 2 *tablespoons flour*
- 2 *eggs, slightly beaten*
- $^1/_3$ *cup dry fine bread crumbs*
- 4 *tablespoons margarine or butter*
- 4 *slices boiled ham*
- 4 *slices fontina or provolone cheese*
- $^1/_4$ *cup dry white wine*
- 1 *($10^1/_2$ ounce) can chicken gravy*

Separate each chicken breast into two portions. Place chicken breasts between two pieces waxed paper; pound to flatten. Sprinkle with salt, pepper and flour; shake off excess flour. Dip into beaten egg, then into bread crumbs. Melt margarine in large skillet over medium heat. Sauté chicken breasts until golden brown, about 3–4 minutes each side. Place in $11^3/_4'' \times 7^1/_2'' \times 1^3/_4''$ baking dish. Place ham slice on each chicken breast; top with slice of cheese. Bake in hot oven (450°), about 10 minutes or until cheese is melted. Brown under broiler, if desired. Combine wine and chicken gravy in small saucepan. Heat, stirring constantly until hot. Serve with chicken breasts.

Spezzatino di pollo alla trasteverina

Trastevere chicken

6 servings

1 ($2^1/_2$–3 pound) chicken,
  cut into 8 pieces
1 teaspoon salt
$^1/_4$ teaspoon black pepper
$^1/_3$ cup flour
5 tablespoons olive oil
$^1/_4$ pound ham, cubed
2 cloves garlic, minced
$^1/_2$ cup dry white wine
2 green peppers, cut into
  rings
1 cup sliced mushrooms
2 medium onions, chopped
1 ($^1/_2$ pound) zucchini,
  sliced
$^1/_2$ teaspoon dried marjoram
1 tablespoon chopped parsley
1 (1 pound) can tomatoes

Sprinkle chicken with salt,
pepper and flour. Heat oil in a
large skillet; brown chicken in
oil. Cook until tender, about
15–20 minutes. Remove; keep
warm. Brown ham; remove;
drain. Stir in garlic and wine;
cook until wine is reduced by
half. Add remaining
ingredients; simmer 8–10
minutes. Add chicken and ham;
stir to blend. Cook until heated
throughout, about 10–15
minutes.

Pollo farcito lessato con salsa di capperi

Chicken with caper sauce

4 servings

$^3/_4$ cup margarine or butter
$^1/_4$ pound chicken livers,
  chopped
1 (4 ounce) can sliced
  mushrooms
$2^1/_2$ cups bread crumbs
$^1/_2$ cup milk
1 tablespoon parsley
$^1/_4$ teaspoon dried oregano
$^1/_4$ teaspoon nutmeg
1 (4–5 pound) roasting
  chicken
2 cups water
1 medium onion, sliced
1 stalk celery, chopped
1 carrot, chopped
$^1/_4$ teaspoon dried thyme
1 bay leaf
2 tablespoons capers
4 anchovy fillets

Melt 4 tablespoons margarine in
large skillet. Brown chicken
livers in margarine; add
mushrooms; cook 1 minute.
Soak bread crumbs in milk;
drain. Add bread crumbs,
parsley, oregano, and nutmeg;
mix lightly. Stuff body and neck
cavities of chicken lightly; truss.
Place chicken in Dutch oven;
add water, onion, celery, carrot,
thyme and bay leaf. Cover.
Cook over low heat until
chicken is tender, about $1^1/_2$
hours. Chop capers and
anchovies together. Melt
remaining margarine in small
saucepan; add capers and
anchovies. Serve over chicken.

Pollo oreganato

Chicken oregano

4 servings

1 ($2^1/_2$–3 pound) chicken,
  quartered
1 teaspoon salt
$^1/_8$ teaspoon black pepper
$^1/_3$ cup olive or salad oil
4 tablespoons lemon juice
1 clove garlic, minced
1 teaspoon finely chopped
  parsley
2 teaspoons dried oregano

Place chicken skin side up, on
broiler pan. Sprinkle with half
the salt and pepper. Combine
remaining ingredients; blend
well; brush on chicken. Broil
under medium heat, 3″ from
heat, basting frequently, about
10–12 minutes. Turn chicken
with tongs, sprinkle with salt
and pepper; baste well.
Continue to cook, basting
frequently, until chicken is done,
or no pink juice appears when
chicken is pricked with a fork.

Filetti di pollo alla piemontese

Piedmontese breast of chicken

4 servings

4 chicken breasts,
  skinned and boned
$^1/_3$ cup flour
1 teaspoon salt
$^1/_4$ teaspoon black pepper
4 tablespoons margarine
  or butter
1 chicken bouillon cube
$^3/_4$ cup hot water
$^1/_2$ cup dry white wine
$^1/_3$ cup grated Parmesan
  cheese
1 tablespoon chopped parsley

Place chicken breasts between 2
sheets waxed paper; pound to
flatten. Place flour, salt and
pepper in large brown paper
bag. Drop several pieces of
chicken into bag at a time;
shake to coat each piece with the
flour mixture. Melt margarine in
large skillet; brown chicken in
margarine. Cook until done,
about 5–8 minutes. Remove
chicken from pan; keep warm.
Dissolve bouillon cube in water.
Stir bouillon and wine into
skillet; blend with drippings;
cook until liquid is reduced by
half. Place chicken pieces on a
heatproof platter; pour sauce
over chicken. Sprinkle with
grated Parmesan cheese. Heat
under broiler until cheese
browns, about 3–5 minutes.
Garnish with chopped parsley.

Anitra brasata con lenticchie

Braised duck with lentils

4 servings

1¹/₂	*cups dry lentils*
	Water
1	*(5 pound) duck*
3	*tablespoons salad oil*
4	*slices bacon, diced*
1	*medium onion, chopped*
1	*medium carrot, chopped*
1	*large stalk celery, chopped*
1	*tablespoon chopped parsley*
¹/₂	*teaspoon dried thyme*
1	*bay leaf, if desired*
1	*cup dry white wine*
1	*teaspoon salt*
¹/₈	*teaspoon black pepper*
¹/₂	*cup chicken bouillon or water*

Wash lentils; place in 2-quart bowl. Cover lentils with water; let soak 2 hours. Prick skin of duck all over with fork. Heat oil in large roasting pan; brown duck in hot oil; remove. Discard fat. Fry out bacon; add onion, carrot, celery, parsley, thyme and bay leaf. Cook over medium heat until onion is transparent; add ¹/₂ cup wine. Return duck to pan. Cover. Roast in a moderate oven (350°) about 1 hour. Meanwhile, drain lentils. Place in large saucepot; cover with water; add salt and pepper. Bring to a boil; reduce heat; simmer until tender, about 15 minutes. Drain well. Pour lentils around duck. Add remaining wine and bouillon. Cover.

Simmer on top of range, over low heat, about 30 minutes or until duck is tender, or no pink juice appears when duck is pricked with fork. Serve hot with the lentils.

Fowl made up many of the favorite dishes of the nobility of ancient Rome. A cookbook of recipes collected by the Roman gourmet Apicius contains at least 40 ways of cooking them. There are recipes for chicken, duck, goose, pheasant and partridge, and for birds we would hesitate to serve today such as stork (stork soup was a particular favorite of the Emperor Nero), crane, peacock, flamingo and ostrich. Paulus of Aegina, a Roman doctor, recommended the brains and wings as the best parts of the ostrich and one recipe recommends boiling the bird with olive oil, vinegar, wine, pepper, mint, celery, sesame seeds, honey and dates for flavoring. As a delicacy Romans served their guests the tongues of flamingoes and even of nightingales. Great care was taken in the raising of chicken for the table. They were fattened on barley soaked in wine and honey, or bread soaked in wine and water. According to tradition, the fattening diet should be started at the time of the new moon. Exactly 20 days later the bird was ready to be eaten. The Italians of the Renaissance ate as lavishly and as exotically as the ancient Romans. The wealthy nobles disdained beef and pork (which they looked down on as peasant's food) and ate only game and fowl. Some of their game dishes would seem strange today, for they ate the meat of bears (which still roamed

the Alps and the hills of the
Abbruzzi), beavers and squirrels.
At the banquets of kings and
princes peacocks and pheasants
would be served, decked out after
cooking in all their plumage with
the tail spread out and the feet
and beak all gilded.
Do you remember the nursery
rhyme about 'four-and-twenty
blackbirds, baked in a pie'. One
cookbook of 1516 gives a recipe
for pie filled with live thrushes
and blackbirds.
First a large pie shell was baked,
with a filling of flour. When the
shell was cooked a hole was made
in the bottom and the flour
poured out. The live birds were
inserted through this hole.
Another smaller pie shell, filled
with flesh from the same sort
of bird as the live ones, was
placed on top and the hole was
then closed up and the pie was
brought to the table. As the pie
was carefully cut, the birds flew
out of the center around the ears
of the guests.

Anitra brasata con olive verdi

Duck with olives

4 servings

> 1   (5 pound) duck
> $^1/_4$ cup olive oil
> 3   tablespoons brandy
> 1   bay leaf
> 3   sprigs parsley
> 1   stalk celery, chopped
> $^1/_2$ teaspoon dried rosemary
> $^1/_2$ teaspoon dried thyme
> $^1/_2$ cup dry white wine
> 1   cup pitted green
>   olives, chopped

Wash and dry duck. Pour olive
oil into heavy roasting pan;
heat. Brown duck on all sides,
pricking with fork in several
places. Remove from heat.
Warm brandy; pour over duck;
light with a match. When flames
subside, add bay leaf, parsley,
celery, rosemary, thyme, and
wine to roasting pan. Cover;
bake in a slow oven (325°) until
duck is tender, about 2–2$^1/_2$
hours. Remove duck from pan;
keep warm. Discard bay leaf,
parsley and celery; skim off
excess fat. Cook until liquid is
reduced to 1 cup; stir in olives.
Serve over duck.

Coniglio dolce e agro

Sweet and sour rabbit

4–6 servings

> 1   cup dry white wine
> 1   clove garlic, crushed
> 1   tablespoon chopped
>   parsley
> $^1/_2$ teaspoon salt
> $^1/_4$ teaspoon dried thyme
> 1   bay leaf
> $^1/_4$ cup raisins
> 1   (3 pound) frozen rabbit,
>   cut into serving pieces or
> 3   pound turkey legs,
>   cut into serving pieces
> 4   slices bacon, diced
> 4   tablespoons flour
> 1   medium onion, chopped
> $^1/_2$ cup beef bouillon
> $^1/_4$ cup vinegar
> 2   tablespoons sugar
> $^1/_4$ cup seedless grapes,
>   halved

Combine wine, garlic, parsley,
salt, thyme, bay leaf and raisins;
heat. Pour over rabbit; marinate
1 hour or longer. If meat is to
marinate more than 4 hours,
refrigerate. Fry out bacon in
large skillet. Remove bacon.
Dry and lightly flour rabbit;
brown rabbit in bacon
drippings. Add onion; cook
over medium heat one minute.
Add marinade. Cover. Cook
over low heat until tender, about
50–60 minutes. Add bouillon as
liquid cooks down. Stir in
vinegar, sugar, grapes; simmer 5
minutes. Remove bay leaf.
Garnish with bacon.

Finoccho al gratin

Fennel au gratin

8 servings

  4 *fennel bulbs*
  3 *tablespoons margarine*
     or butter
  3 *tablespoons flour*
$1/_2$ *teaspoon salt*
$1/_8$ *teaspoon black pepper*
     Dash nutmeg
  2 *cups milk*
  2 *eggs, slightly beaten*
  4 *tablespoons grated*
     Parmesan cheese

Wash and quarter fennel bulbs. Cook fennel in boiling salted water, 6–8 minutes; drain. Melt margarine in saucepan; blend in flour, salt, pepper and nutmeg. Add milk. Cook over medium heat, stirring constantly, until mixture thickens and bubbles. Stir a small amount of sauce into beaten eggs; blend well. Stir egg mixture into hot sauce until well blended. Remove from heat. Stir in 2 tablespoons Parmesan cheese. Place fennel in buttered 8″ square baking dish. Pour sauce over fennel. Sprinkle remaining Parmesan over top. Bake in a hot oven (400°), 10–15 minutes or until golden brown.

Carciofi bolliti

Artichokes

Break stems off artichokes; cut off top third of vegetable. Wash under cold running water. Rub cut portions of artichokes with lemon juice. Drop artichokes into 7–8 quarts boiling salted water. (Do not use aluminum or iron pot). Boil, uncovered, 30–35 minutes. Artichokes are done when leaves pull out easily. Remove; drain upside down. Spread leaves; pull out tender center cone of leaves in one piece. Scrape off and scoop out 'fussy, prickly' portions. Serve hot with melted margarine or butter. Artichokes may also be stuffed and baked. Allow one artichoke per serving.

Carciofi imbottiti

Stuffed artichokes

4 servings

>   4 *artichokes*
>   1 *(8 ounce) can crabmeat, flaked or*
>   1 *cup cooked chopped shrimp*
> $^1/_2$ *cup grated provolone or gruyere cheese*
> $^1/_2$ *cup mayonnaise*
>   1 *tablespoon grated onion*
> $^1/_2$ *teaspoon salt*
>   5 *teaspoons lemon juice*
>   1 *tablespoon salad oil*

Prepare artichokes according to previous recipe. Combine crabmeat, cheese, mayonnaise, onion, salt and 2 teaspoons lemon juice. Spoon crab mixture into center of each artichoke. Arrange artichoke in a shallow baking dish just large enough to hold them, standing upright. Pour boiling water into baking dish to a depth of 1″; add 3 teaspoons lemon juice. Brush artichokes with salad oil. Bake in a moderate oven (350°), about 30 minutes. Serve hot or cold.

Broccoli alla romana

Braised broccoli

4 servings

>   2 *pounds broccoli or*
>   2 *(10 ounce) packages frozen broccoli*
>   4 *tablespoons margarine or butter*
> $^1/_2$ *cup chopped celery*
> $^1/_4$ *cup chopped pimento*
>   2 *tablespoons lemon juice*
> $^1/_4$ *teaspoon salt*
> $^1/_8$ *teaspoon black pepper*

Wash and trim broccoli; cook in boiling salted water 15–20 minutes, or cook frozen broccoli according to package directions. Melt margarine in small skillet; sauté celery 1 minute. Stir in remaining ingredients. Drain broccoli well. Pour margarine mixture over broccoli.

Carote all'anice

Carrots with anise

4 servings

>   1 *pound carrots*
>   2 *tablespoons margarine or butter*
> $^1/_2$ *teaspoon anise seed, crushed*
> $^1/_4$ *cup orange juice*

Peel carrots; cut diagonally into $^1/_2$″ slices. Cook carrots in 1″ boiling salted water about 10–12 minutes or until tender. Drain well; return to pot. Add margarine and anise seed; cook 1 minute. Stir in orange juice; cook 1–2 minutes or until heated throughout.

71

Piselli alla menta

Minted peas

3 servings

- *1 (10 ounce) package frozen peas*
- *1 tablespoon margarine or butter*
- *1 tablespoon mint jelly*
- *1/4 teaspoon dried oregano*

Cook peas according to package directions; drain well; return to saucepan. Add margarine, jelly and oregano. Cook over low heat, stirring constantly just until jelly melts. Serve immediately.

Fagiolini verdi con pancetta

String beans

6 servings

- *2 slices bacon, diced*
- *1 small onion, chopped*
- *2 (10 ounce) packages frozen string beans*
- *1/4 cup water*
- *1/2 teaspoon salt*
- *1/4 teaspoon dried oregano*
- *Dash black pepper*
- *Grated Parmesan cheese*

Fry out bacon in large skillet. Add onion; cook 1 minute. Drain off excess fat. Add stringbeans, water, salt, oregano and pepper; mix well. Cover. Cook over medium heat 5–8 minutes or until stringbeans are tender. Sprinkle with grated Parmesan cheese before serving.

Insalata dei tre fagioli

Three bean salad

6–8 servings

- *1 (17 ounce) can lima beans, drained*
- *1 ($15^1/_2$ ounce) can garbanzo beans, drained*
- *1 ($15^1/_2$ ounce) can kidney beans, drained*
- *1 green pepper, chopped*
- *2 pimentos, diced*
- *3 scallions, chopped*
- *1 teaspoon salt*
- *1/8 teaspoon black pepper*
- *2 cloves garlic, minced*
- *1 (8 ounce) bottle Italian salad dressing*

Combine beans, pepper, pimento, scallions, salt and pepper; mix well. Add garlic to salad dressing; pour over beans. Let salad marinate at least 4 hours in refrigerator.

Asparagi con le erbe

Asparagus with herb sauce

4 servings

- *2 (10 ounce) packages frozen asparagus spears*
- *4 tablespoons margarine or butter*
- *1 clove garlic, cut in half*
- *1 teaspoon chopped chives*
- *1 teaspoon parsley flakes*
- *1 teaspoon lemon juice*
- *1/4 teaspoon salt*

Cook asparagus according to package directions. Melt margarine in small skillet over medium heat. Sauté garlic in margarine; remove. Stir in remaining ingredients. Drain asparagus. Pour sauce over asparagus.

Bagna cauda

Vegetable fondue

8 servings

Vegetables:
- 4 stalks celery, cut into 2″ pieces
- 1 green pepper, cut into 1″ strips
- 2 carrots, cut into 2″ strips
- 1 bunch scallions, trimmed
- 8 cherry tomatoes
- 1 small head cauliflower, broken into flowerets
- 8 asparagus spears, trimmed
- $^1/_4$ pound small whole mushrooms

Dip:
- $^1/_2$ cup margarine or butter
- $^1/_2$ cup salad oil
- 4 cloves garlic, minced
- 1 ($1^3/_4$ ounce) can anchovy fillets, chopped

Bread sticks

Crisp vegetables except mushrooms in a bowl of water and ice for 1 hour; drain; dry on paper towel. Wipe mushrooms with damp cloth. Arrange vegetables on serving tray; cover tightly with plastic wrap; refrigerate until ready to serve. Combine margarine, oil, garlic and anchovies in flameproof casserole or fondue pan. Heat over medium heat. *Do not boil.* Serve immediately with vegetables and bread sticks. Keep sauce warm over candle or on electric hot tray.

Zucchini dolce e agro

Sweet and sour zucchini

6 servings

> 4 tablespoons margarine
>   or butter
> 2 tablespoons salad oil
> 2 pounds zucchini, sliced
> 2 red onions, sliced
> 1 teaspoon salt
> $^1/_4$ teaspoon black pepper
> 2 teaspoons wine vinegar
> 2 teaspoons lemon juice
> 1 clove garlic, cut in half
> 2 tablespoons grated
>   Parmesan cheese
>   Fresh basil leaves

Melt margarine in large skillet; add oil. Sauté zucchini in margarine and oil until lightly browned on both sides; remove. Sauté onion slices in margarine until just slightly softened. Remove. Add salt, pepper, vinegar and lemon juice to skillet; stir to blend; remove from heat. Rub inside of a 2-quart casserole with garlic. Layer half the zucchini in casserole; then a layer of all the onions. Top with remaining zucchini. Pour vinegar mixture over all. Sprinkle with grated Parmesan cheese. Bake in a moderate oven (350°) about 15–20 minutes. Garnish with basil leaves.

Patate alla padella

Fried potatoes

6 servings

    2 (1 pound) cans small
       whole potatoes
    4 tablespoons margarine
       or butter
    1 tablespoon chopped chives
    1 tablespoon diced pimento
  $^1/_2$ teaspoon salt
  $^1/_4$ teaspoon dried oregano
       Dash black pepper

Drain potatoes; dry on paper towel. Melt margarine in large skillet. Brown potatoes in margarine. Stir in remaining ingredients. Cook until heated.

Patate al forno

Baked potatoes

4 servings

    4 large baking potatoes
    4 tablespoons margarine
       or butter
  $^1/_4$ teaspoon parsley flakes
  $^1/_4$ teaspoon dried oregano
  $^1/_4$ teaspoon chopped chives

Thoroughly wash and dry potatoes. Bake potatoes in a hot oven (400°) until soft, about 45–50 minutes. Combine margarine, parsley, oregano and chives. Cut a criss-cross in top of potato; press ends. Top potato with margarine mixture.

Variations:
1. Top potatoes with pesto sauce, page 26.
2. Top potatoes with bacon bits and Ricotta cheese.
3. Top potatoes with chopped scallions and bacon bits.

Cavolfiore alla parmigiana

Cauliflower Parmesan

4 servings

    1 large cauliflower
    4 tablespoons margarine
       or butter
  $^1/_8$ teaspoon dried basil
  $^1/_4$ cup grated Parmesan
       cheese
  $^1/_4$ cup bread crumbs

Wash and trim cauliflower; break into flowerets. Cook covered in a small amount of boiling salted water, 10–12 minutes. Melt margarine in small skillet; stir in basil. Drain cauliflower well. Pour melted margarine over cauliflower; toss lightly. Add grated Parmesan cheese; toss lightly until cauliflower is coated with cheese. Sprinkle bread crumbs over cauliflower before serving.

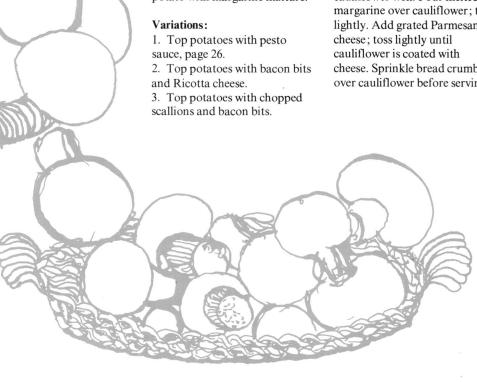

Funghi freschi al funghetto

Sautéed mushrooms

4 servings

- 6 tablespoons margarine or butter
- 2 cloves garlic, minced
- 1 pound small whole mushrooms
- 1 tablespoon parsley flakes
- 1 teaspoon lemon juice
- $^1/_2$ teaspoon salt
- $^1/_8$ teaspoon black pepper

Melt margarine in large skillet over medium heat. Stir in garlic; heat 1 minute. Add mushrooms. Sauté mushrooms, stirring occasionally, 8–10 minutes; stir in parsley. Remove from heat; let stand 3–4 minutes. Sprinkle with lemon juice, salt and pepper.

Melanzane alla parmigiana

Eggplant Parmigiana

8 servings

- 2 large eggplant
- $^1/_4$ cup flour
- 2 eggs, slightly beaten
- 2 cups seasoned bread crumbs
- $^1/_2$ cup salad oil
- 2 (8 ounce) cans tomato sauce or
- 1 (16 ounce) jar marinara sauce
- $^1/_2$ teaspoon salt
- $^1/_2$ teaspoon dried oregano
- $^1/_8$ teaspoon black pepper
- $^3/_4$ pound mozzarella cheese, sliced

Peel eggplant; cut into $^1/_2''$ slices. Dip eggplant slices into flour, then into eggs, then into bread crumbs. Heat $^1/_4$ cup oil in large skillet. Brown eggplant slices in hot oil on one side; turn; brown on other side. Add oil as needed. Drain eggplant on paper towels. Place eggplant in a single layer in a $13^1/_2'' \times 8^3/_4'' \times 2''$ baking dish. Combine tomato sauce, salt, oregano and pepper; pour over eggplant. Arrange cheese slices on top. Cover with foil. Bake in a hot oven (400°), 20 minutes, or until bubbly and cheese is melted.

Cipolle farcite al forno

Baked stuffed onions

6 servings

- 6 large onions, unpeeled
- 1 cup Ricotta cheese
- 1 egg, slightly beaten
- 1 tablespoon parsley flakes
- 1 teaspoon salt
  Dash black pepper
- 1 tablespoon melted margarine or butter

Slice off tops and bottoms of onions; do not peel. Cook in boiling water, 10 minutes. Remove onions; cool; peel. Combine cheese, egg, parsley, salt and pepper, Carefully remove centers from onions. Place a small part of center over hole in bottom of onions. Chop remaining centers; add $^1/_2$ cup chopped onion to Ricotta mixture. Fill onions with Ricotta mixture. Place onions in an 8″ square baking dish. Brush with melted margarine. Bake in a moderate oven (350°), 15–20 minutes.

Porro con scampi

Leek with shrimp

8 servings

- 8 leeks
- $^3/_4$ cup salad oil
- $^1/_4$ cup lemon juice
- $^1/_2$ teaspoon dry mustard
- $^1/_2$ teaspoon salt
- $^1/_8$ teaspoon black pepper
- 1 (4$^1/_2$ ounce) can tiny shrimp

Cut tops off leeks; trim roots. Cut leeks in half lengthwise. Wash thoroughly under running water, holding leaves apart. Cook in boiling salted water about 10–15 minutes. Remove from water; drain well. Place leeks in shallow dish. Combine oil, lemon juice, mustard, salt and pepper; shake well. Pour over leeks. Chill 2–3 hours. Rinse shrimp in cold water. Garnish leeks with shrimp.

Melanzane farcite

Stuffed eggplant

8 servings

- 4 small eggplant
- 4 tablespoons margarine or butter
- 1 small onion, sliced
- 1 clove garlic, minced
- $1/2$ cup sliced mushrooms
- $1/2$ cup grated Parmesan cheese
- 1 tablespoon parsley flakes
- $1/2$ teaspoon salt
- $1/2$ teaspoon dried oregano
- 2 tomatoes, sliced
- 1 tablespoon salad oil

Cut eggplant in half lengthwise. Carefully remove pulp, leaving a shell $1/2''$ thick. Melt margarine in large skillet. Sauté onion, garlic, and mushrooms in margarine until onion is transparent. Chop eggplant pulp; add to onion mixture; cook 3 minutes. Stir in Parmesan cheese, parsley, salt and oregano. Spoon mixture into eggplant shells. Top shells with tomato slices; brush tomatoes lightly with oil. Place shells on baking sheet. Bake in a moderate oven (350°), 20–25 minutes.

Insalata mista

Vegetable medley

6 servings

- 4 tablespoons salad oil
- 1 medium onion, chopped
- 1 clove garlic, minced
- 1 green pepper, chopped
- $1/2$ pound zucchini, sliced
- 1 ($3/4$ pound) eggplant, peeled and cubed
- 1 (1 pound) can tomatoes
- 1 teaspoon dried basil
- 1 teaspoon salt
- $1/8$ teaspoon black pepper

Heat oil in large skillet. Sauté onion, garlic and pepper in oil until onion is transparent. Stir in zucchini and eggplant. Cook about 8–10 minutes, stirring constantly. Add remaining ingredients. Cook, stirring constantly, until heated throughout, about 3–5 minutes.

Slivered carrots and celery, marinated in Italian dressing and finely chopped cabbage topped with creamy salad dressing makes an easy, attractive salad plate.

77

Cappon magro

Genoese salad

8 servings

  1 (8 ounce) package frozen fried flounder fillets
  2 cups (1 pound can) diced beets, drained
$1^1/_2$ cups (1 pound can) mixed vegetables, drained
  2 cups (1 pound can) green beans, drained
$1^1/_2$ cups cooked cauliflowerets, cooled
 $^2/_3$ cup olive oil
 $^1/_3$ cup wine vinegar
 $^1/_2$ teaspoon salt
    Dash black pepper
  1 head Boston lettuce
  1 ($7^3/_4$ ounce) can red salmon, drained
  1 ($4^1/_2$ ounce) can shrimp, drained
  4 hard cooked eggs, quartered
  2 tomatoes, quartered
 $^1/_2$ cup pitted ripe olives
  1 ($1^3/_4$ ounce) can anchovy fillets
    Pesto sauce

Bake fish fillets according to package directions; cool. Combine beets, mixed vegetables, beans, and cauliflower in large bowl. Sprinkle with oil, vinegar, salt and pepper; toss lightly. Chill. Arrange eight lettuce cups on large platter or individual salad plates. Fill each cup with $^1/_2$ cup vegetable mixture. Cut flounder fillets into quarters. Arrange

2 pieces flounder, large flakes of salmon, and shrimp on vegetables. Garnish each serving with 2 eggs quarters, one tomato wedge, several ripe olives, and anchovy fillets. Serve with Pesto sauce.

Pesto sauce:

  1 (10 ounce) package frozen chopped spinach, well drained
 $^1/_4$ cup finely grated Parmesan cheese
  2 tablespoons chopped parsley
  2 tablespoons dried basil
  3 cloves garlic, minced
 $^1/_3$ cup olive oil
  3 tablespoons soft margarine or butter

Place all ingredients in blender; blend smooth, about 15 seconds. Serve with Genoese salad.

Vegetables for salad

Sweets

The tradesmen who came to Venice in the Middle Ages were the first to bring cane sugar to Europe. Sugar remained a luxury item for many centuries. Before the advent of sugar, dishes were sweetened with honey or with some other sweet juice or fruit. It seems that the Italian cooks were the first to discover the secret of preparing first-rate delicacies from cane sugar. Therefore, all through the seventeenth and eighteenth centuries most of the European courts had a French cook and an Italian confectioner. Italians are still very fond of sweets. They do not eat sweets so much as a dessert, however, (fruit is mostly eaten after a meal... it is inexpensive, plentiful, and of excellent quality in Italy), but as a snack in the morning around eleven o'clock and in the afternoon around four and six o'clock. As you pass the coffee bars and pastry shops in Italian cities you will not only see the elderly ladies, wives with children, and young girls busy eating cakes and pies, ices, glazed fruit and other delights, but also just as many men: policemen, priests, students, road-builders, and truck drivers, all doing the same thing. The pastry shop is probably the one place where all Italians come to perfect agreement. They are all there to do the same thing: stuff themselves with the most refined sweets that Italian confectioners can create.

Pere ripiene alla milanese

Stuffed pears Milanese style

6 servings

     6 large pears or
     1 (29 ounce) can pear halves
  $^1/_2$ cup chopped almonds
  $^1/_2$ cup sugar
  $^1/_4$ teaspoon almond extract
     6 maraschino cherries, chopped
  $^1/_2$ cup white wine

Wash pears; cut in half; remove cores. Mix together almonds, 4 tablespoons sugar, almond extract, and chopped cherries. Place pears, cut side up, in 8″ baking dish. Fill centers of pears with almond mixture. Sprinkle with remaining sugar. Pour in wine. Bake in a moderate oven (350°) about 15–20 minutes. Serve hot or cold.

Zuppa inglese

Custard cake

1–9″ layer cake

     4 egg yolks, slightly beaten
     2 cups milk, scalded
  $^1/_2$ cup sugar
  $^1/_3$ cup flour
  $^1/_4$ teaspoon salt
     1 teaspoon grated lemon rind
  $^1/_2$ cup rum
     2 9″ sponge cake layers
  $^1/_3$ cup orange marmalade
     3 tablespoons candied fruit

Combine egg yolks, milk, sugar, flour, salt, and lemon rind; blend well. Strain into heavy saucepan. Cook over low heat, stirring constantly, until thickened, or just before the boiling point. Remove from heat; continue stirring to cool. Cover; chill well. Sprinkle rum onto cake layers. Spread marmalade on top of one layer. Spread $^1/_2$ the custard mixture over marmalade. Place second layer on top; spread with remaining custard. Decorate with candied fruit. Chill thoroughly.

Pesche imbottite alla mandorla

Almond stuffed peaches

6 servings

     1 (30 ounce) can cling peach halves, drained
  $^1/_2$ cup chopped almonds,
  $^1/_4$ cup sugar
     1 tablespoon cherry liqueur
     1 teaspoon grated lemon rind
  $^1/_2$ cup white wine

Place peaches, cut side up, in 8″ baking dish. Mix almonds, sugar, liqueur and lemon rind; fill peach cavities with mixture. Pour in wine. Bake in a moderate oven (350°) about 10–15 minutes. Chill.

Ciliege al vino barolo

Cherries in wine

6 servings

$^1/_3$ *cup sugar*
3 *cup sweet red wine*
1 *(10 ounce) jar (1 cup) red currant jelly*
1 *strip, $3^1/_4''$ orange peel*
1 *cinnamon stick, $2'' \times ^1/_4''$*
2 *(1 pound) cans sour red cherries, packed in water, drained*

Combine sugar, wine, currant jelly, orange peel and cinnamon stick in heavy saucepan. Bring to a boil; stir to dissolve sugar and jelly. Reduce heat; simmer until mixture is well blended and syrupy, about 15 minutes. Add cherries, heat about 2 minutes. Chill; remove cinnamon and orange peel. Serve plain or with custard, ice cream or whipped cream.

Monte bianco

White mountain

4–6 servings

$^3/_4$ *cup sugar*
$^1/_4$ *cup water*
2 *tablespoons butter, softened*
1 *teaspoon salt, or to taste*
2 *cups ($15^1/_2$ ounce can) chestnut puree*
$^1/_2$ *cup heavy cream*
1 *tablespoon sugar*
1 *teaspoon vanilla*

Combine sugar and water in deep 1-quart heavy saucepan. Cook over medium heat, stirring, until sugar is dissolved. Continue to cook without stirring, until syrup reaches temperature of 234° on candy thermometer (soft ball stage). Remove from heat, cool about 5 minutes. Stir butter and salt into chestnut puree. Gradually stir cooled syrup into chestnut mixture. Chill 1 hour. Shape chestnut mixture into one large mountain shape on serving platter or on individual serving dishes. Combine cream, sugar and vanilla; beat until stiff. Spread over mountain shapes to resemble snow. Serve.

Pere al vino rosso

Pears in red wine

4 servings

4 *large firm ripe pears*
1 *cup sweet red wine*
$^1/_2$ *cup sugar*
1 *teaspoon grated orange rind*
$^1/_2$ *teaspoon grated lemon rind*
$^1/_4$ *teaspoon ground cinnamon*
1 *clove*

Quarter, core and peel pears. Arrange in a 8″ baking dish. Heat together wine, sugar, orange rind, lemon rind, cinnamon and clove. Bring to a boil; pour over pears. Bake in a moderate oven (350°) about 30 minutes, or until pears are tender. Serve warm with ice cream or chilled with whipped cream.

Zabaglione

Zabaglione

4 servings

   6 *egg yolks*
   4 *tablespoons sugar*
$^1/_2$ *cup Marsala wine*
      Whipped cream, optional
      Shaved chocolate
   4 *crisp, sugar cookies*

Place egg yolks and sugar in top of double boiler. Beat with egg beater or electric mixer, until light and creamy. Gradually beat in wine. Set into bottom of double boiler over simmering water. Beat until mixture becomes thick, about 3–5 minutes. When beater is lifted, mixture will hold its shape. Do not overbeat. Remove from heat; pour into sherbet or tulip shaped glasses. Top with whipped cream; garnish with shaved chocolate. Serve with a crisp sugar cookie.

According to legend, coffee was first discovered in Ethiopia. A wise shepherd noticed that when his sheep ate the berries of a certain bush they ran and jumped right through the night and showed no sign of being tired. Since the shepherd also wished to remain awake at night so that he could think and meditate, he also ate the berries and found that he not only remained awake, but also that his mind was clear and he could study his books all night. These berries were the beans of coffee plants. The Arabians soon followed the lead of the Ethiopians and ate coffee beans. But they also roasted the beans, brewed a dark drink from them and found that it gave the same results. In 1550 this new drink that the Arabians called 'qahwa' reached Constantinople and, in 1615, the first coffee house in Europe was opened in Rome. Since then, Italy has always been very closely associated with the idea of good coffee. Right after the Second World War, the Italians discovered a new way of making coffee. This method has by now conquered the rest of Europe and much of the world; it is 'espresso'. The principle of 'espresso' is that steam is passed through coffee which is extra-dark roasted and extra-fine ground. Only a couple of swallows are poured into small cups and drunk black with sugar. Sometimes Italians add a frothy topping of steam-heated milk to

make a 'cappucino' (so called because its color and shape resemble the hood of a Capuchin monk's habit). Sometimes cream or whipped cream are used instead of steamed milk. Italians usually drink cappuchino for breakfast, which consists of a roll or pastry eaten while standing at the counter of a coffee bar and reading the newspaper. (Breakfast is not an important meal in most Latin countries.) Italians drink 'espresso' from early in the morning until late at night. They drink it wherever they find it; along the street, on a terrace, in coffee bars, at home, at the station, at the office, in garages, or even in shops and stores. Perhaps it is because the Italians drink so much 'espresso' that they have enough energy to keep active and lively. When the weather is unbearably hot, each coffee bar has a large jar of ice-cold 'espresso' in the refrigerator. There is nothing so refreshing and awaking than a cup of this coffee!

Italians drink it in the afternoon right after their 'siesta' to wake them up so that they can begin the second half of the long Italian day.

Cassata alla siciliana

Mele fredde al barolo

Panna montata 'sorriso di Maria'

Sicilian cake with frosting

1–9" layer cake

- 2 *9" sponge cake layers*
- 2 *tablespoons orange liqueur*
- 2 *cups Ricotta or sieved creamed cottage cheese*
- 1 *cup sugar*
- 1 *teaspoon almond extract*
- $^1/_4$ *cup semi-sweet chocolate morsels, chopped*
- 2 *tablespoons candied fruit, finely chopped*
- $1^1/_2$ *cups confectioners sugar*
- 1 *egg white*
- 1 *teaspoon lemon juice*
- 8 *candied cherry halves*

Cut each sponge layer in half, making 4 layers. Sprinkle three layers with liqueur. Combine Ricotta cheese, sugar, almond extract, chocolate, and candied fruit: mix well. Spread one liqueur-soaked layer with cheese mixture; place another layer on top. Repeat, ending with plain layer. Chill about 2 hours. Combine confectioners sugar, egg white, and lemon juice; mix until smooth. Carefully spread on top of cake. Decorate with candied cherries. Chill thoroughly before serving.

Apples in red wine

6 servings

- 8 *tart cooking apples*
- 2 *cups dry red wine*
- 1 *cup sugar*

Core, peel and quarter apples. Bring wine and sugar slowly to a boil in heavy saucepan, stirring constantly. Add apples. Lower heat; poach apples until just tender, but not mushy, about 20 minutes. Carefully remove apples from syrup with slotted spoon; place in serving dish. Cook syrup briskly until reduced by half. Cool to room temperature. Pour over apples. Serve warm or cool, plain or with whipped cream.

Whipped cream 'smile of Maria'

4 servings

- 1 *cup heavy cream or*
- 2 *cups frozen whipped topping*
- 3 *tablespoons confectioners sugar*
- $^1/_2$ *teaspoon vanilla extract*
- 1 *teaspoon grated orange rind*
- $^1/_4$ *cup marron glaces or*
- $^1/_4$ *cup nesselrode mix*
- 2 *tablespoons grated semi-sweet chocolate*

Whip cream until stiff. Gradually fold in sugar, vanilla, orange rind, and marron glaces. Spoon into 4 sherbet glasses. Sprinkle with grated chocolate. Serve cold.

Pastry

Savoiardi

Ladyfingers

3 dozen

  4 *eggs, separated*
$^1/_8$ *teaspoon salt*
10 *tablespoons sugar*
$^1/_2$ *teaspoon vanilla*
$^1/_3$ *cup sifted flour*

Cut brown paper to fit two cookie sheets. Beat egg whites and salt until foamy. Add 2 tablespoons sugar; beat until soft peaks form; set aside. Beat egg yolks until thickened; gradually beat in remaining sugar and vanilla; beat until very thick and light lemon yellow in color. Sprinkle flour over egg yolk mixture; fold in flour carefully. Fold egg yolk mixture into egg whites. Pipe 3″ long 'finger' shapes on brown paper with pastry tube or spoon, 2″ apart. Bake in moderate oven (350°) 15 minutes or until deep golden brown. Slide paper from cookie sheet. Cool 2–3 minutes. Carefully remove ladyfingers from paper with sharp knife. Cool. Store in airtight container when dry.

Pane di spagna

Sponge cake

2–9″ layers

  6 *eggs, separated*
$^1/_2$ *teaspoon salt*
  1 *cup sugar*
  1 *tablespoon water*
  1 *cup sifted cake flour*
$1^1/_2$ *teaspoons baking powder*
  1 *teaspoon lemon rind*

Combine egg whites and salt; beat until they stand in soft peaks. Gradually beat in $^1/_4$ cup sugar. In another bowl, beat egg yolks until thick and foamy; slowly beat in remaining sugar and water. Sift together flour and baking powder; slowly add yolk mixture; stir in lemon rind. Fold egg whites into egg yolk mixture until well blended. Pour into 2 (9″) cake pans lined with lightly floured waxed paper. Bake in moderate oven (350°) 25–30 minutes or until cake springs back when lightly touched with finger. Allow to cool; then remove from pans and peel off waxed paper.

Cannoli alla siciliana

Sicilian rolls

10 rolls

Filling:

$1^1/_2$ *cups Ricotta cheese*
$^1/_4$ *cup chopped candied fruit*
  3 *tablespoons chopped pistachio nuts or almonds*
2–3 *tablespoons chopped semi-sweet chocolate morsels*
  3 *tablespoons sugar*
$^1/_4$ *teaspoon almond extract*

Rolls:

  1 *cup sifted flour*
$^2/_3$ *cup sugar*
$^1/_4$ *teaspoon salt*
$^1/_4$ *cup Marsala wine*
    Salad oil
  4 *Cannoli tubes or clean, unpainted broomstick pieces, 6″ long*

Combine Ricotta cheese, candied fruit, nuts, 2 tablespoons of the chocolate, sugar and almond extract; stir well. Chill. Sift together flour, sugar and salt. Stir in wine, kneading until firm and elastic. Add a drop or two of wine, if needed; do not allow to become sticky. Continue to knead on floured surface until dough becomes elastic. Place in lightly floured bowl; cover with a damp towel; let stand 2 hours. Roll out on lightly floured board to a rectangle, $22^1/_2$″ × 9″ × $^1/_8$″. Cut into 10 ($4^1/_2$″) squares. Wrap each square diagonally around a cannoli tube or broomstick piece. Moisten surfaces of points which will overlap with a drop of water; press gently to seal. Fry in deep hot fat (350°), 3 or 4 at a time, until golden brown. Drain on paper towel for about $^1/_2$ minute. Using tongs, carefully slip the tubes out of the rolls. Cool. Just before serving, fill with Ricotta filling. Garnish ends with chocolate.

Cenci alla fiorentina

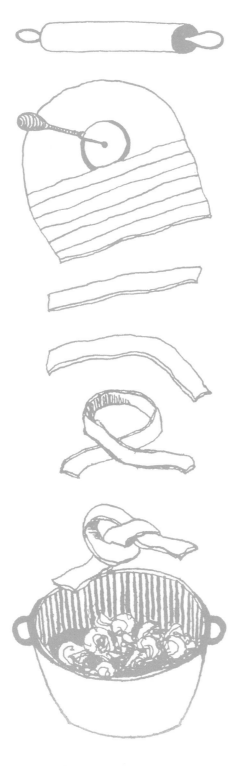

Florentine bowknot cookies

4 dozen

$1^1/_2$ cups sifted cake flour
$1^1/_4$ teaspoons baking powder
 $^1/_4$ teaspoon salt
  1 tablespoon sugar
  3 tablespoons margarine
    or butter
  2 eggs, slightly beaten
    Oil for deep fat frying
  1 cup confectioners sugar

Sift flour, baking powder, salt, and sugar into bowl. Cut in margarine until well blended. Stir in eggs; mix thoroughly. Knead on a floured board until dough is elastic. Let dough rest 1 hour. Divide dough into 4 parts; roll each part to an $8'' \times 10'' \times ^1/_8''$ rectangle. Cut into strips 8″ long and $^3/_4''$ wide. Tie each strip into a loose knot. Fry in hot (375°) oil, 3 or 4 at a time until golden brown. Remove with slotted spoon; drain on paper towel. Sprinkle with confectioners sugar. Serve hot.

St. Joseph, the carpenter husband of the Virgin Mary, is one of the best loved saints among the many dear to devout Italians. He is the patron saint of all honest, hard-working artisans and the protector of the family. The 'festa di San Giuseppe' (Feast of St. Joseph), celebrated on the 19th of March, is the festival of the simple and the poor. In small villages, a great feast is held in the church square on that day. A long table is laid and all the inhabitants bring something to fill it. The poor, the widows and the orphans are the guests. At the head of the table there sits a man, preferably a carpenter, who has at one side a lady and at the other, a child, preferably an orphan. They symbolize the Holy Family. People eat, drink, and dance around a great bonfire. When the feast is over, each person recieves St. Joseph cookies to take home.

Sfinge di San Giuseppe

St. Joseph's cream puffs

8 servings

Filling:

  1 cup Ricotta or cottage cheese
  2 tablespoons semi-sweet chocolate morsels, chopped
  1 teaspoon grated orange rind
  ¹/₃ cup confectioners sugar
  ¹/₂ cup heavy cream, whipped
  1 teaspoon almond extract

Puffs:

  1 cup water
  ¹/₂ cup margarine or butter
  1 cup flour
  ¹/₄ teaspoon salt
  4 eggs
  1 teaspoon grated orange rind
  8 maraschino cherries
    Candied orange peel

Combine Ricotta cheese, chocolate, orange rind and confectioners sugar; blend well. Fold in cream and vanilla. Chill. Combine water and margarine in deep saucepan. Bring to a boil; cook until margarine melts. Quickly stir in flour and salt; beat until dough forms a ball in center of pan. Remove from heat; let stand 5 minutes. Add eggs, one at a time, beating thoroughly after each addition. Beat in orange rind (mixture should be very stiff). Drop mixture from a tablespoon onto a buttered baking sheet. Bake in a moderate oven (375°) 20 minutes or until puffs are firm and crusty. Prick with fork to release steam; leave in oven an additional 5 minutes. Remove from oven; cool. Cut off tops; fill with cheese filling. Decorate with maraschino cherries and strips of candied orange peel.

Zeppole alla napolitana

Neapolitan pastry

makes 1¹/₂ dozen

- 2 cups sifted flour
- 2 teaspoons baking powder
- ¹/₂ teaspoon salt
- 2 tablespoons farina, uncooked
- 2 cups water
- ²/₃ cup sugar
- 3 tablespoons olive oil
- ¹/₂ teaspoon salt
- 1 bay leaf
- 4 egg yolks
- 3 tablespoons Marsala wine
  Olive oil
  Salad oil
  Confectioners sugar

Sift together flour, baking powder and salt; stir in farina. Combine water, sugar, 3 tablespoons olive oil, salt, and bay leaf in large, heavy saucepan. Bring to a boil. Remove bay leaf. Stir in flour mixture all at once, stir over heat until mixture is smooth and forms a ball. Cool slightly. Beat egg yolks into mixture, one at a time, beating well after each addition to form a smooth dough. Add wine; beat until well-blended. Grease a cool marble or plastic topped surface. Place dough on surface. Sprinkle dough with olive oil; cool. Roll dough out to a rectangle 18″ × 12″ with oiled rolling pin. Mark into thirds; fold left third over center; right third over both. Press down with sharp taps with side of hand; give a quarter turn. Lightly sprinkle with olive oil, being sure under surface is oiled. Repeat rolling and folding operation six times. The last time do not fold. Cut in half lengthwise, then cut 8 times crosswise, making 18 strips 2″ × 6″. Slash each strip lengthwise leaving about 1″ at each end connected. Push one end through slash, giving a half twist to dough. Fry in hot (400°) salad oil, 5 or 6 at a time, until deep golden brown. Drain on paper towel. Sprinkle with confectioners sugar.

Pizza

Pizza was discovered by the Neapolitans who had more appetite than money and more imagination than supplies in the cupboard. Pizza was created through the talent for improvisation of Neapolitan bakers who came from the poorer quarters. They knew how to make the best of the little that they had. Pizza is, then, the triumph of the poor man over poverty. It is an ingenious materialization of the zest for existence. Pizza is still precious to Neapolitans. It has brought them fame and fortune. Sophia Loren, who herself comes from one of the poor quarters of Naples, always expresses her pleasure in making her own pizza at home. The basis for pizza is a smooth, elastic, yeast dough. Italians say that it must come from hard Italian wheat. A pizza is not prepared quickly either. It must be kneaded and manipulated; it must be tossed up in the air and caught, twisted around the hand, slapped on the table, rolled, pulled, and handled with all the skill of a juggler at the circus. In some restaurants, this is done right in the middle of the clients. It is only through this play of virtuosity that the dough for a real good pizza is formed. Then this dough is popped into an extremely hot oven. What comes out is an inexpensive light, crispy crust, ready to be filled with equally inexpensive ingredients. The original Neapolitan pizza contained only slices of

Mozzarella cheese, tomatoes, anchovies, garlic and oregano, and a few drops of green olive oil. Today there are thousands of variations of this original pizza; and Italians would not be Italian if they did not let their fantasy run wild in this field. There are pizza with mushrooms and olives, with onions and ham, with mussels and sausages. There are even pizza made of puff dough and of meal dough. These are, however, considered decadent variations of the real yeast-dough pizza.

Pizza is eaten piping hot right out of the oven. The Italian writer Léon Gessi once wrote in a poem about pizza: 'You must face a pizza with one hundred percent trust, as the waiter sets it before you like a freshly blossomed flower, noble, rich, and fragrant. You must give yourself over to it completely. The cheese sizzles and bubbles, it is shining with oil, streaked red with tomatoes, and golden brown. The first glowing hot mouthful dances between tongue and palate; it is a cloud of fragance, it unveils a taste that cannot be clearly defined; it is sometimes both lightly smooth and hot with pepper; it is of a heavy robust softness. Each mouthful that glides down your throat begs to be followed by another'.

Pizza alla napoletana marinara

Neapolitan pizza mariner style

6 servings

Dough:
- 3 ($^1/_4$ ounce) packages yeast
- $^3/_4$ cup warm water
- 3 cups flour
- 1 teaspoon salt
- $^1/_2$ cup water
- 2 tablespoons olive oil

Sauce:
- 1 (29 ounce) can tomatoes, drained and cut into strips
- 4 cloves garlic, minced
- $^1/_4$ teaspoon dried oregano
- $^1/_2$ teaspoon salt
- $^1/_4$ teaspoon black pepper

Dissolve yeast in $^3/_4$ cup warm water; let stand 10 minutes, until foamy. Sift together flour and salt. Stir yeast into flour; add $^1/_2$ cup water. Mix until dough forms a soft elastic ball. Place on lightly floured board; knead about 5 minutes. Place dough in lightly greased bowl; cover. Let rise in a warm place, until dough doubles in volume. Punch down; knead again. Divide dough into 6 equal parts. Roll each section into a 6″ circle about $^1/_8$″ thick. Place on an oiled baking sheet; pinch edge of dough into a collar. Brush each pizza circle with olive oil. Combine garlic and tomatoes; spread on each circle; sprinkle with oregano, salt, and pepper. Bake in very hot oven (450°) 10–15 minutes. Serve hot.

Pizza siciliana

Sicilian pizza

8 servings

Dough:
- 1 recipe Pizza dough (Neapolitan pizza)

Sauce:
- 3 tablespoons olive oil
- 2 medium onions, chopped
- 1 (28 ounce) can tomato puree
- $^1/_2$ cup water
- 2 teaspoons dried oregano
- $^1/_2$ teaspoon dried basil
- $^1/_2$ teaspoon salt
- $^1/_4$ teaspoon pepper
- 8 anchovy fillets
- 8 pitted black olives, sliced
- $^1/_2$ cup Parmesan cheese

Prepare dough as directed in recipe for Neapolitan pizza. Heat 3 tablespoons olive oil; sauté onions in oil, until lightly browned. Carefully add tomato puree, water, 1 teaspoon oregano, basil, salt and pepper; blend well. Simmer covered, about 30 minutes; keep warm. Divide pizza dough into 4 parts; form large 8″ circles on oiled baking sheet or pizza pan. Turn up edges of dough to form a collar. Brush dough with remaining olive oil. Spread $^1/_2$ cup of sauce on each pizza; top with anchovies and black olives. Sprinkle with Parmesan cheese and remaining oregano. Bake in a very hot oven 10–15 minutes. Serve hot.

Pizza siciliana

Calzone imbottito

Stuffed calzone

6 servings

   3 ($^1/_4$ *ounce) packages*
     dry yeast
$1^1/_4$ *cups lukewarm water*
   4 *cups sifted flour*
   1 *teaspoon salt*
   6 *tablespoons softened*
     margarine or butter
   1 *pound mozzarella cheese,*
     sliced
$^1/_4$ *pound hard salami, sliced*
   1 *egg, beaten with*
   1 *tablespoon water*
   3 *tablespoons salad oil*

Dissolve yeast in warm water.
Sift flour and salt into a bowl.
Add yeast mixture; stir to form
a soft dough. Knead on lightly
floured board until dough
becomes elastic and forms a
ball, add water if necessary.
Place in a greased bowl; cover
with a slightly dampened towel.
Let rise in warm place until
doubled in volume. Punch
down, knead 5 or 6 times. Cut
into 6 equal portions. Roll each
portion out into a 9″ circle.
Spread with 1 tablespoon
margarine, leaving 1″ around
edge clean. Divide cheese slices
into 6 equal portions. Stack
salami slices, cut into 6 equal pie
shaped portions. Place 1 slice
cheese on $^1/_2$ of each circle, top
with 1 slice salami. Brush edge
with beaten egg. Fold dough
over filling to form half-moon.
Seal edges with fork. Place on

greased baking sheet. Brush with oil. Let rise, covered with damp towel, for about 1 hour or until doubled in size. Bake in a moderate oven (375°) about 30 minutes or until golden brown. Serve hot.

Ice

Gelato alla vaniglia

The Chinese were probably the first people to invent ices. It was not ice cream, but a kind of sherbet made of fruit mixed with snow. In order to be able to enjoy this refreshing delight in the Summer, they preserved Winter snow in air-tight isolated storage areas. No one can be sure of the exact date of the invention, but it was certainly thousands of years ago. The Greek writer Xenophon writes that 'ices' were eaten in Persia more than 400 years before Christ. When Alexander the Great rode into India more than 300 years before Christ, he saw snow from the mountains isolated and preserved in canals covered with oak tree branches and leaves.

The Romans brought ice from the mountains and packed it in straw and wool because the Emperor Nero liked his fruit juice ice-cold and filtered through snow. But the true art of freezing fruit juice in snow should not to be credited to the Romans but to the Chinese, Indians and Persians. The Arabians and later the Turks, who conquered the Middle East, acquired the art of ice-making from the Persians. In 1191 when the English king and crusader, Richard the Lion Heart, met the Turkish Sultan, Soliman, he was offered fruit sherbet. It seems that King Richard talked about this delicacy for the rest of his life. Italians learned to make ices in the Middle Ages from the Arabs.

Renaissance noblemen enjoyed the refreshing taste of fruit sherbet after the heavy meals at court. Ices were first introduced to France in 1533 by the Italian Bountalenti, one of the cook's assisting at the wedding of Caterina de Medici to the French dauphin. Almost one hundred years later the English tasted ices prepared by Mirra, the Italian cook of King Charles I. Thanks to the Sicilian Procopio, the common man could partake of the pleasure brought by ices. He opened the first ice parlour in Paris in 1670. It was an immediate success and within 6 years there were over 250 cafés in operation in Paris for the sale of Italian ices. The ices were still sorbets prepared according to the Arab-Persian-Chinese recipes: ice, fruit, and water. But Tortoni, owner of one of the Parisian ice parlours, created 'ice cream' in the last half of the 18th century. The Italian, Giovanni Bosio, was the first to sell ice cream in the United States. This began in the last half of the 19th century. Italian ices and ice cream are still considered to be the best in the world; and it makes no difference whether it be the creamy ice cream, or delicious sorbets, or even the heavenly 'granita', half frozen, crushed ice mixed with either coffee or lemon juice. Ice cream is eaten all over Italy but there are two places where the best ice cream in the world can be found: the restaurant

Pappagallo in Bologna (strawberry ice cream such as nowhere else!) and the restaurant Tito del Mole in Viareggio (all kinds of fruit are used: apples, pears, bananas, peaches, melon, etc.). At Tito del Mole, the center of the fruit is used to make ice cream, the ice cream is used to stuff the fruit, and then it is all frozen. The conception of fruit filled with ice cream piled up together with fruit leaves and blossoms and placed in a basket provides a cool sweet delight of which the Chinese, Persians, and Arabs never dreamed!

Vanilla ice cream

2 quarts

6 egg yolks
2 cups whole milk
2 cups heavy cream
1 cup sugar
1 teaspoon vanilla extract

Beat egg yolks until foamy. Combine milk, cream, and sugar in top of double boiler; heat until small bubbles form around sides of pan. Add small amount of cream mixture to egg yolks; then stir yolks into cream mixture in top of double boiler. Cook over simmering water, stirring constantly, until mixture thickens enough to lightly coat a metal spoon. Add vanilla. Strain; cool thoroughly. Pour into two deep metal freezer trays; cover with foil. Freeze until firm but not hard. Chill bowl and beater. Beat with electric mixer on high speed until double in volume. Return to trays; freeze until firm but not hard. Break up; beat again; freeze until firm but not hard. Repeat; freeze until firm about 2 hours.

Gelato di mandorla

Almond ice cream

2 quarts

  1 recipe vanilla ice
     cream page 90
  1 cup almonds
 $^1/_4$ cup sugar
  1 tablespoon almond extract
 $^1/_2$ teaspoon vanilla extract

Prepare recipe for vanilla ice cream; freeze until firm but not hard. Toast almonds in a moderate oven (375°) until light golden brown. Remove from oven; cool. Chop almonds in blender until very fine. Combine ground almonds, sugar, almond extract, and vanilla extract; blend well. Break up vanilla mixture; place in large mixer bowl. Beat with electric mixer on high speed until double in volume. Return to trays; freeze until firm but not hard. Break up; beat again; freeze until firm but not hard. Break up; beat again. Stir in almond mixture; blend well. Freeze until firm.

Granita di limone

Lemon granita

1 quart

  2 cups sugar
  1 cup water
  1 cup lemon juice
  1 cup ice and water
  1 tablespoon finely
     grated lemon rind

Combine sugar and water in heavy 1-quart saucepan; bring to a boil over medium heat, stirring constantly. Cool to room temperature. Add lemon juice, ice and water, and lemon rind; stir until all ice is melted. Pour into two metal freezer trays; place in freezer or freezing compartment. Freeze until almost completely solid. Break up mixture; place in large mixer bowl. Beat at low speed on electric mixer until the consistency of applesauce. Return to trays; freeze one hour. Break up; beat again. Return to trays; freeze until firm, about 1 hour. Serve immediately as a meat or salad accompaniment, or as a dessert.

Granita di caffè con panna montata

Coffee granita sundae

4 servings

$^1/_2$ cup sugar
$^1/_2$ cup water
  3 tablespoons instant coffee
$1^1/_2$ cups ice and water
$^1/_2$ cup chocolate syrup
$^1/_2$ cup heavy cream, whipped
$^1/_4$ cup chopped nuts
  4 crisp sugar cookies

Combine sugar and $^1/_2$ cup water in heavy 1-quart saucepan; bring to a boil over medium heat, stirring constantly. Stir in instant coffee. Add ice and water; stir until ice is melted. Pour into metal freezer tray. Place in freezer or freezing compartment. Freeze until almost solid, about 45 minutes. Break up mixture; place in large mixer bowl. Beat at low speed on electric mixer, until consistency of applesauce. Return to tray. Freeze one hour. Break up; beat again. Return to tray. Freeze until firm, about 1 hour. Scoop coffee granita into 4 sherbet glasses. Pour chocolate sauce over granita; top with whipped cream; sprinkle with nuts. Serve with sugar cookie.

Meringaggio gelato capriccio di dama

Frozen meringue or a lady's whim

8–10 servings

8 eggs whites
$^1/_4$ teaspoon cream of tartar
$^1/_4$ teaspoon salt
3 cups finely granulated
     sugar
1 teaspoon vanilla
1 pint vanilla ice cream
1 pint cherry vanilla
     ice cream
1 pint chocolate ice cream
$^1/_2$ pint heavy cream,
     whipped

Cut brown paper to fit cookie sheets. Mark 3 circles, 8″ in diameter on paper. Beat egg whites, cream of tartar and salt with electric mixer on high speed until soft peaks form. Gradually add sugar; continue to beat at moderate speed until all sugar is added and egg whites form firm peaks. With large-tipped rosette pastry tube or 2 spoons, fill in the circles. Pipe a 1″ high rim on edge of each circle. Bake in a very slow oven (200°) until dry, about 2$^1/_2$ hours. Turn oven off; let meringues cool in oven. Carefully peel circles from brown paper. Place one meringue circle on flat plate; fill carefully with vanilla ice cream. Cover with second meringue; fill with cherry vanilla ice cream. Place third meringue on top; fill with chocolate ice cream. Using small rosette tip on pastry tube, pipe whipped cream between layers, decoratively filling spaces. Pipe rosettes around top edge of chocolate ice cream. Freeze immediately. Serve with currant sauce.

currant sauce
makes 2 $^1/_3$ cups

Heat 2 cups (2 10 ounce jars) red currant jelly in 1-quart heavy saucepan until melted, stirring frequently. Stir in $^1/_3$ cup cherry brandy. Pour into serving bowl, allow to cool. Serve with frozen meringue.

fahrenheit degrees:	*oventemperature term:*
up to 225°	**Cool**
225–275°	**Warm or very slow**
275–325°	**Slow**
350–375°	**Moderate**
400–450°	**Hot**
450–500°	**Very hot**
500	**Extremely hot**
higher	

Kitchen terms

'Al dente'
Literally: to the tooth. This term is particularly used for vegetables and pasta which, though tender, have some bite left in them.

Aspic
A stiff gelatine obtained by combining fish or meat bouillon with gelatine powder.

Au gratin
Obtained by covering a dish with a white sauce (usually prepared with grated cheese) and then heating the dish in the oven so that a golden crust forms.

Baste
To moisten meat or other foods while cooking to add flavor and to prevent drying of the surface. The liquid is usually melted fat, meat drippings, fruit juice or sauce.

Blanch (precook)
To preheat in boiling water or steam. (1) Used to inactivate enzymes and shrink food for canning, freezing, and drying. Vegetables are blanched in boiling water or steam, and fruits in boiling fruit juice, sirup, water, or steam. (2) Used to aid in removal of skins from nuts, fruits, and some vegetables.

Blend
To mix thoroughly two or more ingredients.

Bouillon
Brown stock, conveniently made by dissolving a bouillon cube in water.

Broth
Water in which meat, fish or vegetables have been boiled or cooked.

'En papillote'
Meat, fish or vegetables wrapped in grease-proof paper or aluminum foil (usually first sprinkled with oil or butter, herbs and seasonings) and then baked in the oven or grilled over charcoal. Most of the taste and aroma are preserved in this way.

Fold
To combine by using two motions, cutting vertically through the mixture and turning over and over by sliding the implement across the bottom of the mixing bowl with each turn.

Fry
To cook in fat; applied especially (1) to cooking in a small amount of fat, also called sauté or pan-fry; (2) to cooking in a deep layer of fat, also called deep-fat frying.

Gnocchi
Small balls or dumplings usually made from semolina or potatoes.

Marinate
To let food stand in a marinade

usually an oil–acid mixture like French dressing.

Parboil
To boil until partially cooked. The cooking is usually completed by another method.

Poach
To cook in a hot liquid using precautions to retain shape. The temperature used varies with the food.

Polenta
A thick porridge obtained by boiling corn-meal

Reduce
To concentrate the taste and aroma of a particular liquid or food e.g. wine, bouillon, soup, sauce etc. by boiling in a pan with the lid off so that the excess water can evaporate.

Roast
To cook, uncovered, by dry heat. Usually done in an oven, but occasionally in ashes, under coals or on heated stones or metals. The term is usually applied to meats but may refer to other food as potatoes, corn, chestnuts.

Sauté
To brown or cook in a small amount of fat. See Fry.

Simmer
To cook in a liquid just below the boiling point, at temperatures of 185°–210°.

Bubbles form slowly and collapse below the surface.

Skim
To take away a layer of fat from soup, sauces, etc.

Stock
The liquid in which meat or fish has been boiled together with herbs and vegetables.

Whip
To beat rapidly to produce expansion, due to incorporation of air as applied to cream, eggs, and gelatin dishes.

Alphabetical index

Index by type of dish